God as a Gardener

GOD AS A GARDENER

Exploring Parables Illustrated by Plants

A Bible Study for 21st Century Christians.

Dr. Carolyn A. Roth

Illustrated by Maria Lin

God as a Gardener, Exploring Parables Illustrated By Plants; A Bible Study for 21st Century Christians.

Bibles Used:

Scripture quotations marked (AMP) are taken from the *Amplified Bible*, Copyright © 1954, 1958, 1962, 1964, 1965, 1987 by The Lockman Foundation. Used by permission.

Scripture quotations marked (ESV) are from *The Holy Bible, English Standard Version®*, copyright © 2001 by Crossway Bibles, a publishing ministry of Good News Publishers. Used by permission. All rights reserved.

Scripture quotations marked (KJV) are taken from the *Holy Bible, King James Version*, Cambridge, 1769. Used by permission. All rights reserved.

Scripture quotations marked (NIV) are taken from the *Holy Bible, New International Version®*, NIV®. Copyright © 1973, 1978, 1984, 2002 by Biblica, Inc.™ Used by permission of Zondervan. All rights reserved worldwide. www.zondervan.com.

Scripture quotations marked (RSV) are from the Revised Standard Version of the Bible, copyright © 1946, 1952, and 1971 the Division of Christian Education of the National Council of the Churches of Christ in the United States of America. Used by permission. All rights reserved.

Illustrator: Maria Lin
Book Cover: Maria Lin

Publisher: CRM Publishing, Roanoke, Virginia.

Published in the United States of America

ISBN: 978-1-946919-10-6

Dedication

To my husband, Bruce Roth

Acknowledgements

The following individuals provided advice and support in the preparation of this book:

Bruce Roth, my husband, edited the manuscript and double-checked every Bible reference.

Maria Lin, the Illustrator.

Dr. Ed Bez, President of the Biblical Botanic Garden Society-USA for encouragement and endorsement.

Dr. Gerald McDermott, Anglican Chair of Divinity, History and Doctrine at the Beeson School of Divinity for ongoing encouragement and endorsement.

Why a Bible study about parables illustrated by plants?

God is infinite; he is eternal, everywhere, all knowing, and all powerful. In contrast, mankind lives a short life, i.e., 80 years. We are in a single place at any point in time. We don't know everything there is to know; and, we are relatively powerless. Despite the differences between God and mankind, God wants to communicate with us. In scores of Old and New Testament parables, God used plants to illustrate his nature, spiritual truths about his kingdom, and how he wants us to live.

Interpreting Bible parables and plants in them isn't easy; 21st century society is far removed in time and culture from the Bible's original audience. The distance isn't only chronological, but social, political, and religious. Westernized individuals live in an industrial and technology-driven society. Often, contact with plants grown for food is second or third hand. Individuals don't have an "aha" moment where they understand a parable by its comparison to a plant, i.e., a fig tree, grapevine, or thistle.

To appreciate some parables, individuals need insights into plant life, what the plant looks like, how it grows, and how ancient people used it. We need to know how a plant's characteristics made it an appropriate, even optimal, illustration of God's character and will.

The good news is that many basic plant characteristics—at least for most Bible plants—are fairly stable. This stability helps interpret plants in Bible parables. The current book centers on 24 parables illustrated by plants. I researched these parables and plants to learn why God chose each plant to illuminate the parable's spiritual truth.

Because Old and New Testament parables have different characteristics, I divided the book into a section on Old Testament and a section on New Testament parables. Often the same plants were used in Old Testament and New Testament parables. That's because Christ and other New Testament writers borrowed heavily from Old Testament parables and illustrations.

The book is written for the average church member, rather than for seminarians and clergy. It's for individuals who want a different type of Bible study and those who love plants. This latter group may be individuals who want to grow plants in their home garden or in a church garden. They may be Master Gardeners or members of garden and other nature clubs. Answering the study question, integrated into each chapter, deepens our walk with God. Questions can be pondered alone or discussed with friends in a Bible study group.

Each chapter contains a photograph of an original water-colored illustration of the plant(s). Most Bible plants were identified by Jewish rabbis, historians, and Israeli botanists. When I cited specific plant names, I relied on opinions of Michael Zohary, Professor of Botany at The Hebrew University of Jerusalem, and of Nogah Hareuveni, creator of Neot Kedumim, the Biblical Landscape Reserve in Israel.

Table of Contents

Purpose of Bible Parables

When Christian's think about parables, their minds default to Jesus's parables in the New Testament; however, parables didn't originate with him. Parables are scattered throughout the Old Testament. Seminarians and theologians debate what is and isn't a Bible parable.

Often they deconstruct Bible allegories, metaphors, similes, and fables to determine if each meets criteria for a parable. In contrast to these worthwhile efforts, in this book a parable is a comparison where an image borrowed from the visible world is accompanied by a truth about the spiritual world.

Parables go back to antiquity. In the ancient Middle East, parables were a common method of teaching. They have the following characteristics:

- Attract our attention. We want to know the punch line or end point of the story.
- Stir up or excite us. Often, we remember a parable when another Bible content or a sermon is forgotten.
- Stimulate us to think. We ponder and discuss a parable to understand its meaning. By studying parables, we teach ourselves.
- Inform our opinions. As we add life experiences and mature, we understand and apply parables at different depths.
- Preserve truth. For example, when we recall the parable of the wheat and the tares, we understand that when Jesus comes the second time, the righteous and unrighteous will be separated.

In both the Old and New Testaments, God's spiritual truths were illustrated using plants. Ancient peoples lived close to the land and nature. They depended on plants for food, both for themselves and for their livestock. They grew plants in gardens, i.e., herbs, grains, and grapes. Because ancient people understood plants, they readily interpreted parables illustrated by plants.

A single parable doesn't teach the entire Bible or gospel. It teaches a single point. The first step in understanding the point is to read the entire parable. Don't rush to judgement or conclude immediately that you understand its point. Remember, it is God's divine being and will that we interpret in a parable, not our own preferences. Second, study a parable's context. Review what happened before the parable was told (backstory). Know what occurred subsequent to, or after, the parable was given (outcome). The back story and outcome both aid parable interpretation. Third, although individual parts of the parable develop its truth, not every part contributes to its meaning. Some parts of a parable are there to make the story flow or make it easier to remember. For example, the number of virgins in the parable of the 10 virgins with olive oil lamps doesn't impact the parable's interpretation.

Although a parable has one primary interpretation, it can have many applications. When we apply a parable, we put it into practical use in our lives. Application is personal. My husband and I interpret a parable the same way; but, we apply it differently. Bruce's application reflects his work as a skilled craftsman; while my application is to the church Bible garden.

Section 1
Old Testament Parables

The closest word to parable in the Hebrew language is *mâshâl.*[1] *Mâshâl* translates: to resemble, become like, and compare. In a parable, Jewish writers compared the visible (physical) world to the spiritual world. They used common, every day, visible occurrences to make their point about a spiritual truth. That's one reason ancient writers often used plants in their parables.

The exact number of Old Testament parables is debated. One scholar identified as few as ten, while another identified as many as twenty-six parables. Often scholars hold Old Testament parables to the same standard as those spoken by Jesus. They seem to forget or ignore that Israelite customs and language differed between Old and New Testament times. Further, Jesus was the son of God. Of course his words and actions were superior to those of man.

In Old Testament parables, readers learn about the moral and social life in different periods in Israelite history. We see agricultural practices and religious conditions across time. Old Testament parables attract us by their truth about life. They show man as he was, not an idealized model. Old Testament parables were spoken, seen in visions, or acted out by a cast of characters to include prophets, priests, kings, and an orphaned son. Many were focused locally (Samaria, Jerusalem) and related to a particular event; however, others had national focus, i.e., those of Isaiah and Ezekiel. Several Old Testament parables were fables where plants spoke; others were beautifully crafted poems.

While studying Old Testament parables, I noticed two features which weren't common in the Jesus's parables. First, some parables didn't stand alone; they included another action. For example, Jotham's parable included a curse; while King Jehoash's included a warning. Second, many Old Testament parables were interpreted or explained through actions or outcomes in the same Bible chapter or subsequent Bible chapters. Only rarely was parable's interpretation left to listeners or readers. Whether interpretations were or weren't provided, ancient listeners knew that they were to apply the parable to their lives.

The 12 parables reviewed in the successive chapters in this section aren't an exhaustive list of Old Testament parables illustrated with plants. Some parables were excluded because both the plant and the message were discussed in another parable; i.e., four in the book of Ezekiel and one in the book of Daniel were omitted because the plant appeared previously.

Chapter 1
Balaam's Parable of Aloe Trees

Getting Started: Read Numbers 24:1-9

The parable of the aloe and cedar trees was an oracle spoken by Balaam in Moab. Often the word *oracle* referred to a person, i.e., the oracle at Delphi; however, in this parable oracle meant an authoritative decision or opinion. The third oracle given by Balaam named two trees – the aloe and cedar.

When Moabites saw Moses and the children of Israel approaching their country, they were afraid that the "horde' was going to destroy the land, i.e., cut trees for firewood, consume pasture lands needed for their own livestock. Moabites wanted to turn the Israelites away. The problem was that Moab didn't have a standing army to fight against the Israelites. Until recently Moab was subjects of the Amorites. Moab was only freed from Amorite control when Israelites successfully defeated Sihon, the Amorite king.

The canny King Balak didn't have the military might to stop the Israelites from crossing Moab. He decided to use guile to accomplish his goal. To stop Israelites King Balak king sent for the most renowned seer/diviner in the known world—Balaam. King Balak planned for Balaam to curse Israelites. In ancient times people believed that cursing a person or people could influence their outcome.

Balaam lived about 400 miles north of Moab near the Euphrates River. When Moab envoys first approached him, Balaam refused to accompany them to Moab because God told Balaam not to curse Israelites. Then, the Moabites sent a more distinguished delegation to Balaam and offered him even more money. God allowed Balaam to go with Moabites; however, God warned Balaam that he could only speak the words God gave him.

Every Sunday school child knows what happened next: Balaam was riding a donkey toward Moab when suddenly the normally reliable donkey stopped in the middle of the path. The donkey refused to move forward despite Balaam hitting it with a stick. When the donkey started to talk, Balaam's eyes were opened. He saw an angel blocking the donkey's pathway. Alarmed, Balaam offered to return to his home in Pethor. The angel directed Balaam to go to Moab; but, reminded him speak only words God gave to him.

In Moab, Balaam gave five separate oracles or parables directed at Israelites. Much to King Balak's disappointment, the parables didn't curse Israelites. In fact, Balaam's oracles blessed them! In his third parable, Balaam compared Israelites to aloe and cedar trees planted by God in watered land: "How beautiful are your tents, O Jacob, your dwelling places, O Israel! Like valleys they spread out, like gardens beside a river, like aloes planted by the LORD, like cedars beside the waters. Water will flow from their buckets; their seed will have abundant water. Their king will be greater than Agag; their kingdom will be exalted" (Numbers 24:5-7 NIV).

In this parable the aloe is emphasized, rather than the cedar. In contrast to the aloe of the New Testament, which came from an herbaceous plant, Old Testament aloe came from a tree. In the ancient near east, Old Testament aloe was from the eaglewood tree. Likely, Old Testament traders brought aloe wood from India. The Indian eaglewood is a massive evergreen that grows to 131 feet tall with a trunk (bole) of four-to-eight feet in diameter. Ancient Middle East people believed that the aloe tree was descended from a tree in the Garden of Eden. According to legend, Adam brought aloe tree shoots from Eden and planted them where he and Eve settled.

Aloe is made from agarwood in the eaglewood tree; but, only about 10% of mature eaglewood trees produce agarwood. The fragrant oleoresin that permeates the heartwood of some eaglewood trees is produced by a fungal infection. Once the fungus establishes itself on the tree, the woody trunk turns a deep brown color. The darker the agarwood, the more valuable the aloe. Trees over 50 years produce the best agarwood. Agarwood is harvested, cut into small pieces, and burned. The result is a distinct aroma described as being a cross between sandalwood and balsam.

****

Agarwood gives off a pleasant fragrance or aroma. In the Bible, several places we read that Israelite sacrifices were a sweet aroma to God.

1. Read and summarize (don't just write them out) each verse about what a pleasing aroma to God is:

     a. Genesis 8:21
     b. Exodus 29:18
     c. Leviticus 3:16

2. How did sacrifices change from the Old Testament to post-Jesus New Testament times?

****

Because the eaglewood tree grew in India, likely Balaam never saw one growing in nature. When he included aloe trees in his parable, possibly Balaam referred to the sweet smell of aloe. His point was that the aroma of Israelites was attractive. Yet, this interpretation doesn't reflect Balaam's words about growth of the eaglewood tree. More probably, Balaam heard traders' descriptions of the majesty of aloe-producing trees. Something in or about the Israelite encampment resonated with descriptions Balaam heard of the uprightness of aloe trees.

The Bible story of King Balak recruiting Baalam to curse the Israelites occurred as the Israelites were making their final push into the Promised Land. If Balaam viewed the Israelite encampment immediately after the Israelites left Egypt, he wouldn't have compared them to upright aloe trees. As former slaves, their backs were bent, their heads bowed. In contrast, the current Israelites came

to adult hood as free men and women. They stood upright. They lived in the dry, rugged
Sinai. They were used to standing tall to look into the distance for the first sign of danger to their families or for signs of water and food.

Balaam was smart and knew his craft well. He knew the Israelite history. He knew how they left Egypt. He knew about their 40-year trek in the wilderness. Possibly, Balaam compared the 50 years it took the eaglewood tree to produce mature agarwood (aloes) with the 40 years the Israelites wondered in the desert while they coalesced into a nation. Alternatively, Balaam could have been thinking that only a small number of aloe trees convert to agarwood and sweet-smelling aloes. So too, the children of Israel was a small number, or percentage, of the world's population. Yet, this small nation was unique in being God's chosen people; they were a sweet aroma to God.

Finally, Balaam may have known that aloe trees grew in a variety of environments. Eaglewood trees adapted to different habitats, i.e., rock, limestone, sand, well-drained slopes and ridges, and land near swamps. Similarly, Jacob's offspring lived in and adapted to a variety of living environments, i.e., Canaan, the Nile River delta, the Sinai Desert, and now in Moab.

****

Think about your national culture and society.

1.   Have you seen any events and happenings declared okay or permissible in society that God declared sinful, damaging, or depraved? How are you, or could you be, a sweet aroma to God?

2.   List at least three actions – changes in your life – that would make you more fragrant to God.

     a.

     b.

     c.

****

The spiritual interpretation of Balaam's parable is: what God has declared blessed, man shouldn't curse. The opposite is also true, what God has declared as sinful, damaged, and depraved, man can't declare as valuable and good. Perhaps an application is that we are to grow and fulfill our potential in whatever environment God sets us; like agarwood (aloe), we should be a sweet aroma to God.

If we leave the story of Balaam at this point, we could conclude that Balaam wasn't such a bad guy. After all, he followed God's direction and didn't curse Israelites, But, there is more to the story of Balaam. The Bible recorded that after giving a fifth oracle, Balaam returned home. Possibly, he went back to Pethor; but, Balaam didn't stay there. The Israelites killed Balaam along with five Midian kings in a battle northeast of the Dead Sea (Numbers 31). The Israelites were justified in killing Balaam. He was responsible for advising Moabites and Midianites to use women to seduce Israelite men to sexual immorality and idol worship. This advice led to the slaughter of over 24,000 Israelites.

Final Thoughts:
Only 10% of eaglewood trees produce agarwood. Are you producing a sweet smelling aroma for Christ?

Chapter 2
Trees Crown a King

Getting Started: Read Judges chapter 9

Technically, the parable of the trees is a fable because plants don't speak. In the ancient near east, people were familiar with fables. Hearers knew the fictitious story had a moral that applied to everyday life. Often, they discussed, even argued, the story to figure out its interpretation and application.

Actions of the Israelite judge, Gideon, are important to this parable. Called by God, Gideon was from the tribe of Manasseh; his home was in the Jezreel Valley. Gideon led the Israelites to throw off the seven-year tyranny of the maundering Midianites. One of the many positive characteristics of Gideon was his refusal to be king over the Israelites after he defeated them. His words were, "I will not rule over you, nor will my son rule over you. The Lord will rule over you" (Judges 8:23 NIV). Gideon had 70 sons by his wives and one son, Abimelech, by his concubine. Abimelech lived with his mother's people in Shechem. Abimelech's name means "my father is king."

After Gideon's death (c. 1122 BC), Abimelech negotiated with his uncles and men of Shechem to crown him king. Abimelech and a group of paid adventurers murdered Gideon's legitimate sons with the exception of the youngest, Jotham. Abimelech's coronation occurred at the great oak tree at Shechem. At this site Joshua had made a covenant between God and the Israelites. He recorded God's decrees and laws in the Book of the Law of God (Joshua 24:25-26). In the approximately 250 years between Joshua (c. 1375 BC) and

Gideon's deaths, these Israelites moved from belief that God was their king to putting their confidence in an earthly king.

****

Before Israelites entered the Promised Land, God instructed them to kill all Canaanites.

1. How could the situation among Jotham-Abimelech-Shechemites been avoided?
2. Identify times when you blatantly disobeyed God's instructions. How did those times work out for you?

3. Identify what you would or could do differently. Don't you wish hindsight was foresight?

****

When Jotham gave this parable, he was heart sick. Not only had his father, the stable person in his life, died; but, his half-brother murdered every other brother. Although the Bible doesn't say so, likely Abimelech seized all of Gideon and his brothers' lands. Jotham, legitimate son of Gideon, was left with nothing. On top of everything else, the men of Shechem and surrounding areas proclaimed Abimelech king! Jotham was outraged by the injustice perpetrated by Abimelech and the same people Gideon fought to free from the rapacious Midianites.

On the day that Abimelech was crowned, Jotham climbed to the top of Mount Gerizim and loudly proclaimed this parable:

> Listen to me, citizens of Shechem, so that God may listen to you. One day the trees went out to anoint a king for themselves. They said to the olive tree Be our king. But the olive tree answered, Should I give up my oil, by which both gods and humans are honored, to hold sway over the trees? Next, the trees said to the fig tree, Come and be our king. But the fig tree replied, Should I give up my fruit, so good and

sweet, to hold sway over the trees? Then the trees said to the vine, Come and be our king. But the vine answered, Should I give up my wine, which cheers both gods and humans, to hold sway over the trees? Finally all the trees said to the thornbush, Come and be king. The thornbush said to the trees, If you really want to anoint me king over you, come and take refuge in my shade; but if not, then let fire come out of the thornbush and consume the cedars of Lebanon! (Judges 9:7-15 NIV).

Jotham didn't stop with a parable, he included a curse. Jotham's curse was that if the people acted honorably toward Gideon who fought for them and rescued them from the Midianites, then Jotham wished them joy in their new king. However, if they acted dishonorably, then let fire come out of Abimelech and consume the citizens of Shechem and Beth Millo and let fire come out of the two towns and consume Abimelech.

After giving the parable and curse, Jotham fled south to Beersheba. Jotham made his home at Beersheba because he feared Abimelech.

****

Have you ever wondered how Jotham's life turned out?

1. Read Romans 3:23. How does Romans 6:23 apply to Jotham' life?

2. Do you believe that Jotham ignored any of God's instructions?

3. What is your answer to the age-old question of why bad things happen to good people?

****

The thornbush agreed to be king of the trees with the caveat that other trees rest in its shade. Resting in a king's shade was a common euphemism for a king caring for the people he ruled and for the people submitting to the king's will. The thornbush said if the other trees refused to rest in its shade, then its fire would consume the cedars of Lebanon. Essentially, the thornbush threatened that if it was made king, and then subjects refused support, it would destroy them. In Jotham's parable, Abimelech was the thornbush who agreed to be king after all honorable men declined. The cedars of Lebanon symbolized the Israelite people over whom Abimelech ruled.

Jotham's choice to use the thornbush as a symbol of Abimelech's lack of qualifications to be king demonstrated that he knew how trees grew. The thornbush was known commonly as the atad.[2] It is larger than all, or most, fruit trees native to Israel. In the wild, it can grow 30–35 feet tall; consequently, it grows as a tree more often than a bush. Branches are dense and intertwined. Sometimes, branches dropped downward, almost touching the ground. When this happens, sunlight can't reach the area beneath the bush and little grows there. Each leaf has a pair of thorns. One hard thorn is straight, while the other is hooked. The thorns depicted how harshly King Abimelech would treat his subjects. Further, no local citizen, trader or traveler could rest safely beneath the thorn tree because of the dangers of low hanging branches and thorns.

The thornbush root system is deep and wide spreading. Frequently, thornbush roots leach all nourishment from the surrounding soil.[3] For fruit trees, i.e., olive, fig, pomegranate, to grow successfully, farmers must first remove all thornbushes before planting fruit trees. Although Abimelech was king, his subjects wouldn't be able to grow under his kingship. Abimelech would leach resources from his subjects in much the same way that the thornbush leached nutrients from soil. Jotham knew that other trees and smaller plants couldn't grow under thornbushes.

In Israel, thornbushes produce flowers between March and October. The fruit is yellow and small, less than one inch in diameter. Each fruit contains a large stone (pit) surrounded by fleshy pulp. Fruit is best eaten green. In no way does the quality of the thorn bush's fruit compare favorably to the olive, fig, or grape. In ancient Israel, thornbush fruit was only eaten by people who were very poor or in time of famine. I have a thornbush in the church Bible Garden. The small fruit tastes similar to an unripe apple.

The overall worldly or physical interpretation of this fable/parable was that a) Abimelech was a lesser man than Gideon, b) Abimelech's reign would be disastrous for the Israelites whom he ruled, and c) fruit of Abimelech's reign would be less than the present situation where the Israelites were ruled by God and his appointed judges.

Thorn tree   Maria Lin

The spiritual interpretation of Jotham's parable and this horrific situation is that when we move ahead of God's timing, the outcome is sub-optimal, if not disastrous. God's choice for the first human king of the Israelites, King Saul, wasn't crowned for another 70 plus years. At this time (immediately post Gideon) in Israelite history, God's plan was for Israelites to have judges as leaders. When the Israelites went their own way and crowned a king, the result was inferior to God's plan for them.

****

Why do you think that Abimelech wanted to be king?

1. Did Abimelech's love of power separate him from God or was some other sin occurring in his life? If another sin, what do you think it was?

2. God had a plan for Abimelech's life which Abimelech negated by his actions. What are some alternate ways that Abimelech could have acted, along with possible outcomes?

3. Read Romans 6:23. How does Romans 6:23 apply to Abimelech's life?

****

After three years of Abimelech's kingship, God sent an evil spirit between Abimelech and the Shechemites. We aren't sure how the evil spirit worked. Perhaps, after becoming king, Abimelech had time to think about his status. True, he was undisputed king because he killed all opposition; however, his backers were mercenaries. Further, the townsmen who supported him were the type of men who condoned the murder of Gideon's sons. How secure was his throne? How likely was it that his sons would succeed him as king? Townsmen over whom King Abimelech ruled may have had second thoughts. They remembered Gideon's words that God should rule over them, not a man. They couldn't trust a man who slaughtered his 70 brothers. Some Shechemites ambushed and robbed people who passed by Shechem, thus, thumbing their nose at Abimelech and his "power" to keep the peace.

A man named Gaal and his brothers moved into Shechem. Gaal was a Canaanite. Many townsmen turned from King Abimelech and started to follow Gaal. While Gaal and his followers were eating and drinking, they cursed Abimelech. Abimelech heard about their disrespect and attacked Gaal and Shechem. Gaal was ousted from Shechem; however, Abimelech proceeded to attack Shechem. About 1000 men and women took refuge in the Shechem tower. Abimelech ordered his men to gather branches from Mount Zalmon. He piled branches against the tower and lit them with fire. All 1000 people in the tower died from the fire, heat, and smoke inhalation. The Bible didn't identify the types of trees or branches used to burn the Shechem tower; but, likely the thornbush was included among them.

Not satisfied with destroying Shechem, King Abimelech and his army went to Thebez and captured the town. He attacked Thebez's tower. A woman inside the tower dropped a millstone that cracked Abimelech's skull. Abimelech didn't want it known that a woman killed him so he persuaded his servant to kill him. When Abimelech's followers saw that he was dead, they went home; thus, ended the short three-to-five- year reign of the first king of Israel.

Jotham's curse came true. Fire came out of the thornbush (Abimelech) and destroyed the citizens who supported him. Out of the towns Abimelech ruled, came fire—in this case rebellion—that caused King Abimelech's death

Final Thoughts:
Do you believe that Jotham's parable and curse had an impact on the outcome of this story?

Chapter 3
Transient Plants and Wicked Men

Getting Started: Read Psalm 37

Some Old Testament parables tell a complete story, i.e., trees crowning a king. Others are short. Sometimes they even appear terse. Whether long or short, each parable has a spiritual message that unfolds through ideas, events, or natural objects in the physical world. In Psalm 37 King David included three parables of one-to-two verses each. These short parables compared wicked, ruthless men to plants.

As we read Psalm 37, we imagine an older and wiser King David. He isn't any longer the brash aspirant to Israel's throne or a newly crowned king. This King David has seen a wide range of events and people in his lifetime. He acknowledged his sin of having Uriah killed so he could marry Bathsheba. He knew his daughter was raped, and subsequently dealt with the murder of Crown Prince Amnon. King David was deposed as Israel's king and fought a heart-breaking battle to regain his throne. God, who David adored, told David that his hands were too bloody to build God's temple.

King David wrote psalms before and after he became King of Israel. Many were written to praise God or they were prayers to God. In contrast, Psalm 37 is directed toward all who will listen.[4] David wrote this psalm to praise God and to teach individuals who heard it. In Psalm 37, some of the 40 verses are discrete thoughts while others are two-verse couplets. All are loosely organized around the theme that wicked men perish while good men prosper. David averred that God views righteous (good) versus wicked individuals differently.

David had some friends and many loyal followers; but, over his lifetime he experienced plots from many enemies. In Psalm 37 he told righteous men "Do not fret because of evil men or be envious of those who do wrong; for like the grass they will soon wither, like green plants they will soon die away" (Psalm 37:1-2 NIV). David was very clear about the outcome of wicked men "But the wicked will perish: The Lord's enemies will be like the beauty of the fields, they will vanish" (Psalm 37:20 NIV).

Because fields, flowers, and grass are reviewed with New Testament parables, I am going to focus on David's third plant parable in Psalm 37. David wrote: "I have seen a wicked, ruthless man spreading himself like a green laurel tree. But he passed away, and behold, he was no more; though I sought him, he could not be found" (Psalm 37:35-36 ESV).

****

When you see wickedness and ruthlessness actions,
you can identify them.

1. Define each word:

      Wickedness:

      Ruthlessness:

2. How are these words similar and how do they differ?

3. Mentally, identify who in your circle of friends is wicked? Who is ruthless?

****

In this parable King David compared a man to a tree that flourished. The man's activities, although wicked and ruthless, were successful. They spread beyond himself, his family, his community, and sometimes even his city. His actions were cruel and without pity. He didn't care how he achieved his wealth and influence. This is the man who took property from widows and orphans. But, and this "but" is reassuring: this merciless man disappeared. The parable doesn't tell the reader if he died or if his wickedness caught up with him. Perhaps, someone even more wicked brought him down. David's parable tells readers only that the man "was no more." David even looked for the wicked man – perhaps David wanted to know if he was still wielding his power, but, David couldn't find him.

****

Ponder whether or not your trust God with events in your life.

1. If you trust God, how does your life show it?

2. If you do not trust God, how does your life show it?

3. Any changes you want to make in how you act?

****

David's green bay tree is known to Americans as the bay laurel tree. Characteristics of the bay laurel tree make it a fitting comparison to the transience of wicked, ruthless men. In Israel, laurel trees are called the sweet bay laurel because bay leaves come from the tree. During David's reign laurel trees grew wild from Mount Hermon in northern Israel southward through the Jezreel Valley and into the Judean Mountains. Today most laurel trees are 6-12 feet tall; however, in ancient Israel laurel trees grew to 60 feet. In Israel the laurel tree is an evergreen, retaining green leaves year around. One way to identify it is to bruise or cut a leaf and smell the sweet aroma; the aroma is of a bay leaf.

One of the most important attributes of laurel trees—and one that King David apparently knew—was that laurel trees thrive where they are planted. They tend to wilt and even die if they are moved repeatedly. Ideally, gardeners plant laurel trees and allow them to grow in place. Further, laurel trees are sensitive to cold and frost.

laurel branch   Maria Lin

When King David wrote that he saw wicked and ruthless men who flourished like a green laurel tree in its native soil, he was thinking of a mature laurel tree with a broad canopy and numerous branches. This tree never suffered setbacks from being transplanting. Likewise, prosperous, wicked men never seemed to have setbacks. In spite of their seemingly charmed lives, David noted that later he looked for these wicked men. They were gone. David concluded that wicked men don't endure; they have no staying power. Perhaps, like a laurel tree, wicked men can't tolerate adversity—to include cold weather, frost, and transplanting. The laurel tree and a wicked man flourished, but, only in a narrow environment.

The spiritual focus of this parable is: righteous men and women's incentive to act right (using biblical moral-ethical standards) comes from knowing that ultimate power on earth and in heaven is in the hands of a just God. Even if righteous persons don't experience worldly prosperity, they are rewarded in heaven for how they acted on earth. In a later Psalm, David averred that the righteous flourish like a palm tree and like a cedar of Lebanon planted in the Lord's house (Psalm 92:12-14). Righteous men and women bear fruit in old age and stay both fresh and green.

In the three parables in Psalm 37, King David went beyond identifying the puzzle of seeing wicked individuals prosper. David advised not to fret when evil men (and women) prosper because fretting leads to evil. When David said evil, he meant anger, resentment, or mimicking wicked and ruthless men's business practices. Instead, we should refrain from anger and hope in the Lord. Hoping in the Lord means we shoulder bad as well as good times from God. We accept cares and joy.

****

Are there alternatives to anger and resentment at seeing evil and ruthless individuals prosper? What are some of these alternative that you could exhibit?

****

In contrast to King David's parables that speak to the transience of wicked men, probably each us have seen wicked men and woman who have thrived their entire career, even life. Was David wrong in verses 35-36? What did he mean? MacDonald[5] wrote that King David may have been stating a general principle. He noted that Holy Scripture often makes sweeping statements; it describes a general, or normal, outcome of spiritual laws. Exceptions don't disprove the overall principles.

Final Thoughts:
When we concentrate on flourishing in the garden where God plants us, we don't obsess about whether or not ruthless

Chapter 4
Parables of Vineyards

Getting Started: Read Psalm 80:8-13 and Isaiah 5:1-6

Do you want your heart to break? Then, read these two parables. Learn about Israelites' rejection of God. Although written at two different times in Israelite history and by two different men, both parables are a cry of anguish from God to his chosen people. Both identify God as a gardener and Israelite as his vineyard. A vineyard and vine are synonyms with the nation of Israel (both Northern and Southern Kingdoms).

After the death of King Solomon, the Israelite kingdom divided (c. 930 BC). The Northern Kingdom, called Israel, included 10 tribes: Ephraim, Manasseh, Dan, Zebulun, Asher, Naphtali, Issachar, Gad, Reuben, and Simeon. Some of the greatest Israelite prophets, Elijah and Elisha, lived in the Northern Kingdom. The Southern Kingdom was known as Judah. At times, Judah included both the tribes of Judah and Benjamin. At other times, Benjamin seemed more aligned with the Northern Kingdom. Levite towns were located in both Israel and Judah; but, for the most part the Levites were associated with Judah and the Jerusalem temple.

The first Northern Kingdom king introduced idol worship, which was embraced by much of the population. God sent prophets, Elijah, Elisha, Amos, Hosea, etc. to warn Israel that their idol worship and flaunt of God's laws would cause God to reject them. All calls for repentance were ignored. After 200 years (c. 722/721 BC) Assyria conquered the Northern Kingdom. Most of its inhabitants were exiled throughout the Assyrian Empire.

In the Southern Kingdom, Judah, descendants of King David ruled until 586 BC. Despite prophets, i.e., Isaiah, Jeremiah, Ezekiel, warnings and calls for repentance, Judah turned from God to worship a myriad of idols. Jerusalem fell to the onslaught of the Babylonians. Most citizens not killed were taken captive to Babylon.

****

In their pride both the Northern and Southern Kingdom forgot that God was their hedge. They believed that their armies were protection for their borders and for their populations.

1. What do you believe is your protection from the world? Money? Gated community? Job? Etc.

2. Overall, what do we as Americans believe are protections against foreign oppressors? How are our beliefs similar and different from antient Israelites?

3. How could you increase your life's security?

****

Bible scholars believe that Psalm 80, a lament, was written in response to the fall of the Northern Kingdom. The psalmist was from the family of Asaph, a Levite singer, poet, and head of King David's choir. Likely, Psalm 80 was written in Jerusalem from where the Northern Kingdom collapse was closely observed:

> You transplanted a vine from Egypt; you drove out the nations and planted it. You cleared the ground for it, and it took root and filled the land. The mountains were covered with its shade, the mighty cedars with its branches. Its branches reached as far as the Sea, its shoots as far as the River. Why have you broken down its walls so that all who pass by pick its grapes? Boars from the forest ravage it, and insects from the fields feed on it (Psalm 80:8-13 NIV)

Isaiah's parable used a similar comparison of a gardener who planted a vineyard. Instead of lamenting the downfall of the Northern Kingdom, Isaiah identified the fate of Judah. The song of the vineyard is a love song that described God's love and care for his people, how they rejected him, and ultimately God's punishment of Judah.

> I will sing for the one I love a song about his vineyard: My loved one had a vineyard on a fertile hillside. He dug it up and cleared it of stones and planted it with the choicest vines. He built a watchtower in it and cut out a winepress as well. Then he looked for a crop of good grapes, but it yielded only bad fruit. "Now you dwellers in Jerusalem and people of Judah, judge between me and my vineyard. What more could have been done for my vineyard than I have done for it? When I looked for good grapes, why did it yield only bad?

> Now I will tell you what I am going to do to my vineyard: I will take away its hedge, and it will be destroyed; I will break down its wall, and it will be trampled. I will make it a wasteland, neither pruned nor cultivated, and briers and thorns will grow there. I will command the clouds not to rain on it (Isaiah 5:1-6 NIV)

On the physical or natural level, vineyard parables included preparing and protecting a vineyard. Parts of Canaan were ideally suited for vineyards and grape production. A single cluster of grapes could weigh 24 pounds. Remember, the spies sent by Moses into Canaan (Number 13:23)? They returned with one cluster of grapes that required two men to carry. Grapes became a principle export of Israel under King Solomon. Hillsides, where wheat didn't grow well and cattle couldn't be pastured, were ideal sites for vineyards. In the Northern Kingdom, the hill country in Manasseh and Ephraim produced grapes and grape production occurred in Naphtali in the far north of Israel. In Judah, the area around Hebron, with its many hill, was perfect for vineyards. In En Gedi, vineyards were plentiful.

Usually, ancient Israelites enclosed vineyards with fences. Often farmers dug a ditch around the vineyard. The earth from the ditch was thrown to the inner side of the ditch. Then, fence posts and thorny plants were placed on the berm. At other times, a wall of stones or sun-dried mud took the place of the earthen fence with its thorny plants. Boulders and rocks were plentiful in Canaan. Large boulders were removed from the vineyard area and used for stone fences. Small stones weren't removed from the soil; their presence encouraged the soil to retain moisture, needed by vineyard's soil.

Both the psalmist and Isaiah referenced vineyard fences. The psalmist asked God why he broke down vineyard walls and removed its hedge so that all who passed could pick the grapes. Further, boars from the forest could ravage the vineyard. Isaiah prophesied that if Judah didn't repent, God would remove their walls and the country would be trampled. Briers and thorns would grow in former vineyards.

God built a watch tower to protect his vineyard Israel. For centuries Israelite vineyards had booths and watchmen who protected the vineyard from marauders. The booth became the watchman's home for the summer months. Sometimes a simple booth was constructed on a high spot where the watchman could view the entire vineyard.

Frequently, watchman's booth was made of tree branches and boughs, and provided shelter from the rays of the sun. At other times a more durable tower was constructed, especially if the watchman's family live with him during the summer months. These towers were from ten feet to an occasional forty feet tall. In the winter months the watch tower was deserted. The watchmen that God set over his vineyard, Israel, were first judges and then kings; nonetheless, Israel was a theocracy with God as their ultimate king. Israelites' first allegiance was to be to God.

In Isaiah's parable the vineyard was planted, "with the choicest vine" (Isaiah 5: 2). Farmers traded for the best vines available or purchased the highest quality vines that they could afford. As the vine grower devoted himself to the vineyard and grapes, God devoted himself to the children of Israel. He did everything possible to select good vines, protect them, and promote good growth in them. Yet, when God

Vineyard   Maria Lin

anticipated a yield of good grapes from his vineyard, he got only bad grapes. A Northern Kingdom prophet summed up what God wanted from his people: for them to act justly, love mercy, and walk humbly with him (Micah 6:8). God expected a yield of righteousness. Instead the people were disobedient, rebellious, and idolatrous. God was so disturbed that he asked: "What more could have been done for my vineyard than I have done for it?" (Isaiah 5: 4 NIV).

****

God judges our actions

1. Imagine God is viewing your life's actions (and he is). What does he see doing right?

2. Imagine God is viewing your life (and he is), what does he see you doing wrong, in inconsistent with God's statutes?

3. Is your life in the correct righteous-unrighteous proportions? What could you change to improve this proportion?

****

The spiritual interpretation for both Psalm 80 and Isaiah 5:1-6 is that there are consequences to sin and both the Northern and Southern Kingdoms would experience those consequences. The consequence of Israel and Judah's sins was that God abandoning them. God removed his protection from both kingdoms with the result that both was attack and ruined. In their pride both kingdoms forgot that God was their hedge. They believed that armies were protection for their borders and for their populations.

In these two parables we can learn a second spiritual lesson: God's judgment is proportional. After becoming a nation separate from Judah, immediately Israel turned to idol worship, i.e., Jeroboam I set a golden bull in Dan and Bethel and told Israel's citizens that the bulls were the gods that brought them out of Egypt. Over the next 200 years, most of the nation's population repudiated God. In response, God allowed the nation of Israel to fall and most of its people to be exiled from the land. Many of Judah's leaders and population rejected God through idol worship, but, some kings, i.e., Hezekiah and Josiah, initiated reform and returned to worship of God. Although God removed his protection from Judah and Jerusalem, he provided a way for these Jews to return to Jerusalem, rebuild the temple, and reestablish themselves as a nation.

Final Thoughts:
Nations are made up of citizens.
Were God's expectations of Israelites
too high?

Chapter 5
God as an Evergreen Tree

Getting Started: Read Hosea 14:8

The parable of the green tree is one of the Bible's miniature parables. Not only is it brief, but it tends to be obscure. Obscure parables allow the Holy Spirit to call forth prayerful study, so parables are fully interpreted.[6] When Hosea spoke the parable of the evergreen tree, it stimulated the ears of the people who heard it. Today, we read the parable and visualize the majesty of a green tree.

Hosea was a prophet to the Northern Kingdom (Israel). Hosea lived and prophesized during the middle of the eighth century BC, during the final tumultuous days of Israel when six kings reigned in 25 years. Most were murdered by their successors with only one effective transition from father to son. The major tribe of the Northern Kingdom of Israel was Ephraim. Frequently, Hosea referred to the Norther Kingdom as Ephraim.

Generally, we remember Hosea because God directed him to marry an adulterous woman. Many scholars consider Hosea and Gomer's story a parable in and of itself. Hosea's interactions with Gomer are contained in only the first three chapters of his book. In the other eleven chapters, Hosea implored the Northern Kingdom to repent so that God could heal their waywardness.

****

The title of Hosea chapter 14 is: "Repentance to bring Blessing"
(NIV)

1. If you are as old as I am, you heard the saying "Love means that you never have to say you are sorry." Do you think that this statement is accurate. If the statement is true, then I never have to tell God I'm sorry.

2. Look up the definition of repentance in the dictionary. Is repentance more than telling God you are sorry?

3. Can the "Repentance to bring blessing" statement be true? How does repentance bring blessings?

****

Hosea averred that Israel's disloyalty to God and idol worship was spiritual adultery. He identified Assyria as the source of God's judgment on the Northern tribes. Because Hosea came from the Northern Kingdom, he knew every pride and perversion of royalty and citizen alike. Yet, Hosea spoke of God's love, mercy, and forgiveness.

In the first three verses of Hosea chapter 14, Hosea exhorted Israel to do three things:

- stop sinning by worshiping idols made by their hands
- ask God to forgive their sins
- return to worshiping God.

Hosea assured Israel that Assyria can't save them, nor can war horses (from Egypt). God alone can save Israel.

The next four verses (Hosea 14:4-7) are a beautiful outline of how God will heal Israel's waywardness if only the nation will return to God. When we read the verses, our hearts rejoice at what God – even at this late time – is willing to do for Israel. God's healing is expressed using plant metaphors:

- God will be like the dew and Israel will blossom like a lily
- Like a cedar of Lebanon, Israel will send down roots and send up new growth
- Israel's splendor will be like an olive tree

- Israel's fragrance will be like a cedar and men will again live in its shelter
- Israel will flourish like grain and blossom like the grape vine
- Israel's fame will be like wine from Lebanon.

After assuring the Israelites that God can and will heal Israel, Hosea offered a parable. Initially, I read the parable in the New International Version (NIV) Study Bible; however, I disagreed with the NIV translation of the tree as a pine tree. The pine tree that grows in Israel is named the Aleppo (Syria) or Jerusalem pine. Although an evergreen, normally the Aleppo pine is short-lived (70-100 years). It has a shallow root system. The pine tree is a poor example, and perhaps a poorer translation, of the tree in Hosea 14:8.

Other Bible translations identified the tree as a cypress tree (AMP, RSV). Characteristics of the cypress make it a more likely candidate for a comparison with God. Here is the parable: "O E′phraim, what have I to do with idols? It is I who answer and look after you. I am like an evergreen cypress, from me comes your fruit" (Hosea 14:8 RSV).

In verse 8, God told the Northern Kingdom he has nothing to do with idols. God is separate, different and apart, from idols and images that people make with their hands. God wants the northern tribes to forget about idols, to clear them from their minds. God is the one, the only one, who can answer prayer. God can look after the nation and people in it. Whether a golden calf at Bethel or an image under a tree, idols have nothing to do with the living God.

****

Idols are what we place ahead of God.

1. What idols do you worship in your life, i.e., spouse or children?

2. In your Bible, read Exodus 20:3-4 and 1 Corinthians 10:14. What did God command about idols?

****

Cypress, green tree   Marcia Lin

In the Old Testament God revealed in many places and ways that he wanted to protect his chosen people and make their lives better, i.e., lead them in green pastures and beside quiet waters (Psalm 23:1-2), heal, guide, restore, and comfort them (Isaiah 57:18), and give them the kingdom forever and ever (Daniel 7:18). Perhaps, nowhere is God's caring so forthrightly and succinctly presented as in Hosea 14:8. He told Israel that he, not an idol, answers them and looks after them. He is like a green cypress tree. From God comes Israel's fruit, both their food and their righteousness.

The wild cypress tree of Israel was commonly called the Mediterranean cypress. The cypress remains green year around. The cypress tree is large, strong, durable, and full of resin which acts as a barrier against water seeping into the wood. Cypress trees are enduring, typically living at least 1000 years. Ancient Middle Eastern peoples viewed the cypress as a symbol of immortality. In the Bible, the cypress-wood ark carried eight individuals through the raging flood that destroyed life in the then known world. Not surprisingly, the cypress tree was associated with immortality through God's divine will.

****

Where will you spend your immortality?

Probably, you have heard many times, that we will all have immortality. The question is where each of us will spend that immortality: in heaven or in hell. I'm positive where I'm going to be.

Are you sure where you will be? Read the following verses then answer the question.

- Ephesians 2:8-9
- Acts 4:12
- Romans 10:9-10

****

On the Mediterranean cypress, loosely hanging branches grow from the central column in a whorl. Branches are rounded and have small elongated needles for leaves. Cypress tree branches and stems grow close together. These growth patterns plus year-around needles means that people, who take protection under a cypress tree, have little exposure to rain or snow. Likewise, the thickness of branches means travelers who rest under the cypress are rarely exposed to the sun. What a wonderful analogy of how God wanted to protect Israel, i.e., from the sun, rain, and snow.

Instead of brightly blooming flowers, the cypress tree produces cones. The same tree produces both male and female cones. On the Mediterranean cypress, pollination of female cones occurs in the summer. After pollination, the female cone's green ovules turn to seed. Usually, fertile cones turn brown and drop to the ground the year following pollination. God promised that if Israel would follow him, the country would once again be fertile, green and grow.

The parable's spiritual interpretation is that man-made idols aren't immortal; they aren't even alive. They are statues, man's creations. Some have ears but they can't hear. Some have mouths but they can't speak. Having a head is not the same as having a brain and mind. Immortality, including long life for an individual or a nation, comes only from God.

I read through the Bible several time; but, perhaps, unlike you, I never paid attention to Hosea 14:8. Hosea is a relatively murky book which other than the parts about Hosea and Gomer doesn't seem all that intriguing. But, this is the only place (that I know of) where God compared himself to a living organism. We know that God is enduring like the mountains, the soil, and the ocean.

In Hosea, God liken himself to something alive, as he is alive. That living organism was a tree with a lovely smell and which was disease resistant. Although ancient people used the cypress tree to symbolize immortality, God doesn't just symbolize immortality; he is immortal. By likening himself to a green cypress tree, God compared himself to a tree that lived so many more years than a man's lifetime. To man with his short life of 80 years, the cypress tree seemed immortal.

Final Thoughts:
An evergreen tree is alive. God is alive.
Where are you going to be alive
eternally?

Chapter 6
Crackling Thorns and Fools

Getting Started: Read Ecclesiastes 7:6

The parable of crackling thorns is short, contained in one verse. A comparison is made between the physical world and a spiritual truth. It attracts our attention, excites us, stimulates thought, and preserves truth. The crackling thorn parable was meant to be experienced by the ears. Indeed, we hear both crackling thorns as they burn and the loud boisterous laughter of fools.

The parable of cracking thorns was recorded in the book of Ecclesiastes. Ecclesiastes is part of the wisdom literature of the Hebrew people. Bible scholars aren't sure who wrote Ecclesiastes. Some suggested that Solomon authored the book. Others proposed that a citizen rather than a king was the writer and that Ecclesiastes was written long after the reign of Solomon. The writer referred to himself as "Teacher" (Ecclesiastes 1:1).

The focus of Ecclesiastes is that individuals should enjoy the life that God gives them. The author questions how mankind can live meaningfully, purposefully, and joyfully in the relatively short time allocated to each individual. Simultaneously, the Teacher answers his question by saying that a full life can be had if individuals place God at the center of all activities, i.e., work, family, church. The Teacher concluded that life under God was good, despite its multiple puzzles, paradoxes, and conundrums.

****

Name three things about a non-Christian lifestyle appeal to you.

1.

2.

3.

Do you want this lifestyle? Why or why not. If you are not sure reflect back to what you learned in Chapter 5.

****

When Bible-readers were asked what they learned from reading Ecclesiastes, most answered with some variation of, "meaningless, meaningless, all of life is meaningless." With that answer, some proceeded to identify another Bible passage that told a more compelling story, stated a clearer principle for a Godly life, or prophesized an exciting end-time event. Yet, the Teacher's sometimes sly and thinly perceived wisdom gives direction for life to individuals who want to learn wisdom.

This parable that the Teacher wrote compared a fire of crackling thorns to the laughter of fools. In ancient Israel, cooking fires were in outer courtyards or inside homes. The time of year determined where the fire was located. In hot weather it was in the courtyard. In cooler or cold weather, the fire was located inside the home to add warmth. Many poor Israelites cooked over a simple hole in the ground (a fire pit) with rocks around it. Others had ovens, either inside the home or in the courtyard. Sources of fuel included wood, animal dung, and thorn bushes.

The parable of crackling thorns is included in a chapter titled: The Contrast of Wisdom and Folly (ESV). Despite the chapter's name, the parable addressed folly, rather than wisdom. The parable reads:

"Like the crackling of thorns under the pot, so is the laughter of fools. This too is meaningless" (Ecclesiastes 7:6 NIV).

When the Teacher concluded the parable with, "This too is meaningless," he linked the laughter of fools to burning thorn bushes. A closer look at the word "meaningless" showed that it means "futile" or "has no purpose." Synonyms are "pointless and ineffective;" while the antonym is "useful."

****

How could you go about acting less foolish and more wisely?

1. Where or how would you start this process?

2. What would you have to give up?

3. What would you have to or want to add to your already busy life?

****

The thorn plant in Ecclesiastes 7:6 is the thorny burnet commonly called the prickly burnet. The Hebrew word for crackling is *qôwl* (*qôl*), an unused root word meaning a voice or sound.[1] In present-day Israel, thorny burnet can be found from northern Mount Hermon through Eilat, in the far southern desert. Like fools and their laughter, thorny burnet is widespread.

When individuals used thorny burnet plants as cooking fuel, three plant characteristics are important: First, although the burnet plant grows in dense clumps, it isn't a good source of cooking heat. Dry thornbushes burn readily and thorn heat flairs up quickly, but the fire dies down just as quick. Thornbushes provide no sustained heat to cook a meal or bake bread as heat generated from wood. Similarly, the laughter of a fool occurs readily; but, soon ends as reality sets in, the amusing event passes, or the joke is over.

Thorny burnet

Maria Lin

Second, in Israel thorny burnet flowers bloom at the end of the rainy season, February–April or earlier in Israel. Mature female flowers are set in four-to-five joined petals. The top of the petals are covered tips of sepals (modified leaves set around the petals) which makes the female flower resemble a covered pot. These flower "pots" are numerous. In a fire, flower "pots" produce a small explosion. Although a thorny burnet fire may snap, crackle, and pop, and be pleasing to the ears, the sound adds nothing to the heat. Similarly, a foolish person rejects the Lord for earthly pleasure and laughter, both of which are ultimately meaningless.

Third, skin on fingers and arms can be pricked by plant thorns when the thorny burnet is added to a fire. Similarly, when foolish individuals laugh at us—even when the laughter is short lived—the laughter pricks us. True, we can look back and reflect on whether or not their loud laughter was appropriate or valuable; but, in the moment, the laughter hurts. This use of thorny burnet in the parable demonstrates how ridicule and laughter can hurt us and influence how we live our lives.

****

Ridicule and laughter can hurt us.

1. People who make fun of others act foolishly. What does the fool say about God (Psalm 14:1)?

2. Is God with you when you are the butt of foolish laughter? Where is God at that time (Psalm 14:5)?

3. If you wanted God to be with you – so you can ignore when others make fun of you—what can you do?

****

Ecclesiastes 7:6 is the only Bible verse which identified the thorny burnet; however, since the days of Adam and Eve thorns and thornbushes have played a role in agriculture and in parables. In the Bible, thorny plants were often associated with desolation and ruin. Enjoyment such as alcohol and carousing with friends leads to foolish laughter; but it also leads to desolation and ruin. Sometimes life on earth seems long, as year after year goes by. Yet, these seemingly long years are short when compared to eternity. So, too is the seeming happiness of foolish decisions. For a short time, they may bring gaiety; but, in the long run, which includes eternity, they provide little joy.

Final Thoughts:
I feel so inadequate when individuals make fun of me for my faith. Probably, I should feel sorry for them.

Chapter 7
The Cedar and the Thistle

Getting Started: Read 2 Chronicles 25:17-18

The parable of the cedar and the thistle is technically a fable. In it one plant speaks to another, i.e., the thistle to the cedar of Lebanon. Some Bible commentators called this parable a riddle because certain words King Jehoash spoke were difficult to interpret. When King Jehoash of Israel delivered the parable to King Amaziah of Judah, he also gave a warning to Judah's king.

The context includes previous events in both the Northern Kingdom (Israel) and the Southern Kingdom (Judah). Jehoash was king of Israel, which included ten Israelite tribes that settled in the north of Canaan and the three tribes east of the Jordan River. Although an idol worshipper, King Jehoash visited the prophet Elisha and wept over Elisha's ill health. Because God had compassion on Israel, he allowed King Jehoash to defeat the Aram army in battle three times. Israelite towns, captured by the Arameans, were returned to Israel.

In Judah (composed of the tribes of Judah and Benjamin), Amaziah was king. Initially, King Amaziah followed God. He determined to finish subjugating Edom, started by his father King Joash. King Amaziah mustered an army of 300,000 fighting men from Judah and Benjamin. In addition, he hired 100,000 soldiers from Israel, paying them upfront a hundred talents of silver.

Then, a man of God (a prophet) came to King Amaziah. The prophet told King Amaziah that if he took Northern Kingdom soldiers with him into battle, God would cause him to lose the battle with Edom.

King Amaziah believed the prophet. He sent the Israelite soldiers home, letting them keep the money he paid them. The Israelites soldiers were furious. They wanted the opportunity to fight in the battle and to plunder rich Edomite lands. Plunder, not payment for fighting, was the major source of riches for soldiers in the ancient Near East. While King Amaziah was fighting the Edomites, these same Northern Kingdom soldiers raided towns that belonged to Judah. They killed three thousand people and carried off great quantities of plunder.

King Amaziah led his army to the Valley of Salt where they killed 10,000 Edomites outright. Then, captured another 10,000 Edomite soldiers who they killed. When King Amaziah returned from battling the Edomites, he brought back Moabite idols. King Amaziah set the idols up in Jerusalem, bowed down to them, and burned sacrifices to them.

****

Idolatry is always wrong.

1. Why did King Amaziah bring the Moabite gods/idols back to Jerusalem and worship them?

2. Why consult a God of a conquered people?

3. Do you have any gods/idols that you carry around from place to place that replace God?

****

God was angry with King Amaziah for his idol worship and sent a prophet to him. The prophet asked the king, "Why do you consult this people's gods, which could not save their own people from your hand?" (2 Chronicles 25:15 NIV). While the prophet was speaking, King Amaziah interrupted him and told the prophet that if he continued to speak he would be killed. The prophet stopped, but told King Amaziah that God would destroy the king because he worshipped idols and wouldn't listen to the prophet's counsel.

After consulting with his advisors, King Amaziah sent a message to King Jehoash to meet him face-to-face. In other words Amaziah challenged Jehoash to battle. Likely, the reason for Amaziah's challenge was Israel's plunder of Judah's lands while Amaziah was fighting the Edomites. Because a king's subjects paid taxes, they expected their king to keep them safe. As king of Judah, Amaziah couldn't ignore Israel's murder of 3000 individuals or their plunder of Judah's land.

Rather than immediately agreeing to Amaziah's challenge, Jehoash sent a message back to Amaziah in the form of a parable and a warning:

> A thistle in Lebanon sent a message to a cedar in Lebanon, Give your daughter to my son in marriage. Then a wild beast in Lebanon came along and trampled the thistle underfoot. You say to yourself that you have defeated Edom, and now you are arrogant and proud. But stay at home! Why ask for trouble and cause your own downfall and that of Judah also? (2 Chronicles 25:18-19 NIV).

In the parable, King Jehoash of Israel referred to Israel and himself as a mighty cedar of Lebanon. In contrast, he named King Amaziah and Judah as a lowly thistle. By identifying himself and Israel as cedars of Lebanon, King Jehoash co-opted for Israel the name "cedar of Lebanon," a term used to refer to the Israelite nation from before they entered the Promised Land.

To King Jehoash, King Amaziah's challenge was as ludicrous as if he asked for Jehoash's daughter to wed his son. In ancient times, sons of kings married daughters of kings only if the kings were equals in terms of land and wealth. Clearly, King Jehoash perceived that there was no equality between himself and the King of Judah. He was the mighty cedar of Lebanon and a much more powerful king than Amaziah.

King Jehoash went further in his insult to King Amaziah by giving King Amaziah a warning: King Jehoash identified King Amaziah as arrogant because he defeated the Edomite; but, King Amaziah was asking for trouble if he persisted with the challenge to Israel. A future battle would result in King Amaziah and Judah's downfall. King Jehoash was convinced that even though King Amaziah won a decisive victory over the Edomites, he and his army were more experienced. After all, they won three major battles against Aram, a noteworthy adversary. Further, Judah and Benjamin were composed of only two tribes versus the ten tribes of Israel. Israel had more fighting men than Judah.

In the Bible, about 20 different words are related to some type of prickly or thorny plant. In Jehoash's parable, the Hebrew word for thistle is *choâch* or *hoah* and is associated with the *Scolymus* genus of plants.[3] When King Jehoash named King Amaziah a thistle, possibly he was thinking of the spotted golden thistle.

There is a huge difference in size and characteristics of a thistle and a cedar tree. In contrast to the spotted golden thistle which grows a maximum of three feet tall, the cedar can grow 120 feet and has a main trunk diameter of six-to-eight feet. The spotted golden thistle is an annual herbaceous plant that grows in abandoned fields and ditches and along paths and trails. Essentially, thistles are weeds. In contrast, cedars are evergreen trees that are beautiful in winter and summer. The cedar of Lebanon grows in mountainous and rocky soil; its roots extend deep into the ground. Cedars grow slowly; it takes centuries to produce a majestic cedar tree.

Spotted golden thistles have little if any value to man or animals. Leaves are oblong and prickly. For the most part, even livestock avoid the thistle. Yellow flowers bloom May to August, but have no noticeable scent. Cedar wood is durable, free from knots, and easy to work. The heart wood is warm red and beautifully grained. Cedars exude a gum or balsam which gives the tree an aromatic scent in which people take delight. Most insects dislike the smell and taste; consequently, they don't attack cedars. Cedar wood is resistant to fungal disease so doesn't readily develop dry and wet rot.

An expert botanist, King Solomon knew the cedar tree's characteristics. For God's temple, Solomon used cedar trees from Lebanon rather than any tree in his own country, i.e., sycamore or box tree. Given the different characteristics and value of the two plants, who would want to be characterized as a thistle when the alternative was the cedar of Lebanon?

Golden thistle

Cedar of Lebanon

The spiritual interpretation of the parable King Jehoash offered to King Amaziah was that King Amaziah's pride would lead to his destruction. King Amaziah didn't comprehend that his success over Edom was due to God being on his side. After King Amaziah's decision to worship Edom idols and not allow God's prophet to advise him, God left King Amaziah. Now, he would go into battle against King Jehoash and Israel with no divine assistance.

****

Silently, we glory in accomplishment.

1. Has your high self-assessment ever caused you to think more highly of yourself in a church situation?

2. Has your low self-assessment ever caused you to think more highly of yourself in a church situation?

3. How can we have a realistic assessment of our abilities?

****

The two kings met in battle at Beth Shemesh, a town in Judah near the border of Dan. The Bible gave no details about the battle, i.e., number of men on either side; however, in the battle King Jehoash captured King Amaziah. King Jehoash took King Amaziah to Jerusalem. There, King Jehoash tore down 600 feet of Jerusalem's wall in an area that made Jerusalem most vulnerable to attack. Jehoash took gold and silver from God's temple along with the palace treasures. King Jehoash returned to Samaria with hostages from Judah. Some scholars believe King Jehoash took King Amaziah with him to Samaria. Only after King Jehoash died was King Amaziah returned to Judah.

King Amaziah lived about fifteen years after King Jehoash died. From the time Amaziah turned away from God, Jerusalem leaders conspired against him. At some point, King Amaziah fled Jerusalem, fearing for his life. Jerusalem conspirators sent men to Lachish and assassinated King Amaziah. King Amaziah's life and rule became as insignificant as a thistle which King Jehoash compared him to in the parable.

Final Thoughts:
"When pride comes, then comes disgrace,
but with humility comes wisdom"
(Proverbs 11:2 NIV)

Chapter 8
Poem of a Plowman

Getting Started: Read Isaiah 28:24-29

The parable of the plowman is a two-stanza poem. The first stanza focuses on plowing the ground for planting; second stanza on threshing a crop. The poem ends with praise to God who taught mankind how to plant and harvest. Finally, the parable's interpretation unfolds.

Because the Hebrew language and Hebrew poetry differs from English, native English-speakers can't appreciate the memory cues in this Hebrew poem. We don't remember it in the same way that we remember, even memorize, Burns, Longfellow, and Whitman's poems.

The parable of the plowman is an agriculture parable that resonated with farmers. The writer, Isaiah, was an urban agriculturist. Although Isaiah lived most of his life in Jerusalem, the content of Isaiah's book demonstrates a sure knowledge of ways crops were planted, cultivated, and harvested.

Isaiah saw visions and prophesized during the reigns of Kings Uzziah, Jotham, Ahaz, and Hezekiah. From Jerusalem he saw the final days of the Northern Kingdom. He warned the Southern Kingdom (Judah) that her sins would bring captivity. At the same time, Isaiah assured hearers that a remnant of Jews would be restored to Jerusalem and Judah.

The immediate context for the parable of the plowman begins in Isaiah chapter 28, verse 9. The country's leaders mocked Isaiah; but, more importantly, they mocked God. The leaders asked: Who is God to try to teach us? Are we babies? Are we newly weaned children? No! They were adults and didn't need detailed instructions from God, i.e., "Do and do, do and do, rule on rule, rule on rule, a little here, a little there" (Isaiah 28:10 NIV). The rulers in Jerusalem boasted they entered a covenant with death and the grave; thus, when a foreign nation invaded them, they wouldn't be touched (Isaiah 28:14-15).

****

Most Christians speak to God and believe God speaks to them.

1.   Several years ago, I was praying and believe strongly that God spoke to me in my prayer. When I shared my experience with a non-Christian friend, her comment was ridicule, i.e., there was that something mentally wrong with me because I heard voices.

2.   When you pray about certain topics, do you believe that God speaks to you (in some way) to give an answer? What are sources of God speaking to you?

3.   What do your mediation/contemplation/prayers consist of? Do you ever take time for God to speak to you as well as speaking to God?

****

According to Isaiah, reality for both Israel and Judah would be different
than what they expected. Neither country was prepared militarily or spiritually for foreign invasion, an invasion that God allowed in judgment for their rejection of him and his laws. Foreign soldiers would engulf Israel and Judah. Instead of God's words through a prophet, citizens would hear a foreign language spoken on foreign lips. Protection from death and the grave would be annulled. The people will be beaten down by the invaders, taken captive, and exiled. Judah's power politics, i.e., reaching out to Egypt for protection from northern invaders, won't work.

Isaiah implored the Israelites to hear him four times, i.e., listen, hear, pay attention, and hear what I say (Isaiah 28:23). Isaiah wasn't speaking to hear his own voice; nor was he speaking his own thoughts and words. Instead, Isaiah gave God's message, a message vital to Judah's health and security:

Listen and hear my voice; pay attention and hear what I say. When a farmer plows for planting, does he plow continually? Does he keep on breaking up work the soil? When he has leveled the surface, does he not sow caraway and scatter cumin? Does he not plant heat in its place, barley in its plot, and spelt in its field? His God instructs him and teaches him the right way.

Caraway is not threshed with a sledge, nor is the wheel of a cart rolled over cumin; caraway is beaten out with a rod, and cumin with a stick. Grain must be ground to make bread; so one does not go on threshing it forever. The wheels of a threshing cart may be rolled over it, but one does not use horses to grind grain. All this also comes from the Lord Almighty, whose plan is wonderful, whose wisdom is magnificent (Isaiah 28:24-29 NIV).

****

Who teaches mankind?

1. Do you believe—really believe—that God taught farmers how to prepare soil, plant seeds? Or did farmers learn by a trial-and-error evolutionary process?

2. What are the implication of believing that God taught farmers the process versus trial and error?

3. Do you think that in the 21st century, God teaches mankind new technologies or is mankind's current learning processes trial and error?

****

The parable of the plowman identified three activities a farmer used, i.e., breaking up the soil, sowing seed, and threshing the crop. The order of these three actions comes from God; they couldn't be implemented in a different sequence and still achieve an optimal harvest. Further, each class of seed requires its own soil, sowing method, and threshing.

Breaking up the soil. A farmer plowed his land; but, at a point when the soil was soft and ready to receive the seed, the farmer stopped plowing. Too fine plowing and repeated plowing wastes the farmer's time and contributes to topsoil erosion and loss. Over plowing influenced the Dust Bowl in the 1930s in central United States.

Sowing seed. A farmer knew the best sowing techniques to get an optimal crop. He sowed caraway and scattered cumin. The knowledgeable farmer even knew that hard grain (wheat, barley, spelt) seeds needed to be sowed differently. He didn't mix seeds together. He planted grain seed in their own plots aware that they matured at different rates and were harvested at different times.

Threshing crops. The farmer knew how to thresh his crops to obtain a maximum yield. He beat the caraway with a rod (flail); however, cumin was extracted with a stick. Wheat, barley, and spelt were threshed using sledges or threshing wheels rotated by a donkey or ox.

In the parable of the plowman, two herbs were named. Although New International Version Bibles translate the first herb as caraway, other Bibles (AMP, ESV, KJV) translate this herb as fitches, dill, or fennel. Because the second herb, cumin, was translated uniformly in different Bibles, it is used as the prototype herb. Barley will be contrasted with cumin because of barley's historic significance to the Israelite nation.

Although cumin is an herb, it has the distinction of being the second most popular spice in the world. Probably, cumin originated in the Nile River Valley. Israelites may have taken cumin seeds with them when they left Egypt. According to Isaiah, ancient Israelites scattered cumin on the top of prepared soil in the spring. Cumin seeds need a lot of water, but not a soggy environment. Growing conditions for cumin seeds parallel how Israelites—particularly the Northern Kingdom—over-indulged themselves. Just as some water is good for cumin seeds and seedlings, some wealth and leisure are good for a nation, but excess leads to sin.

Cumin plants benefit from a little crowding. Ideally, they are grown in groups or clumps. Plants support each other, keeping stems from bending over and touching the ground. Similar to a cumin plant needing the support of other plants to grow optimally, Northern and Southern Kingdoms, i.e., all 12 tribes of Israel, needed each other for optimal growth. When Israel and Judah separated they didn't have each other for support. Both nations became vulnerable to outside attack.

Cumin seeds are ready to harvest when pods turn brown and dry. When this happens, pods open and spill their seeds onto the ground. Often, pods don't dry all at once, but, need to be harvested at different times throughout the season. Like cumin seeds, the sins of the Northern and Southern Kingdom matured at different rates. The Northern Kingdom was destroyed almost 200 years before Jerusalem.

In contrast to the herb cumin, barley is a grain. For Israelites, barley was a major food staple for several reasons. First, barley was less expensive to purchase than wheat. Second, barley was drought-resistant and grew in both alkaline and saline soils; consequently, barley grew in the diverse habitats of the Promised Land. Third, under favorable conditions, barley ripened in as few as 60–70 days, a shorter time than wheat matured. In Israel, winter barley was sown in November and December and harvested in April or early May. Israelites were so closely associated with barley that Midianites referred to them as "barley cakes" (Judges 7:13).

By the time Isaiah prophesized, Israelites used two-hand wooden plows with an iron point on the end; the iron point turned over the ground. Plows were pulled by an ox and guided by the farmer. Barley seeds were dropped in rows or furrows and covered by harrowing (or smoothing) the soil over seeds. Once ripe, barley stalks were cut using a scythe; then transported to the threshing floor in wagons or in large baskets. Wealthy farmers had their own threshing floors, but more often a threshing floor was shared by a village or town, i.e., they were publicly owned and located outside of the town wall. When Isaiah prophesized, there were four methods of threshing, i.e., stick, animals, threshing sledge, and wheel.[7] The most common and effective method to thresh barley was with the sledge. A sledge was a platform made from two wooden boards. The front was upturned so it would not jam

Cumin

Barley

Maria Lin

against the floor when pulled by animals. On the sledge bottom, hard stones and later iron was embedded to break the barley kernel from the stalks.

In order to achieve security for their land, citizens had to recognize and abide by God's rules just as planting herbs and grains followed certain agrarian rules. Unfortunately, in Israel and Judah both leaders and citizens rejected God and God's requirements for national and personal holiness. There was little, if any, justice in either Israel or Judah. The result was God's judgement on each nation and its people. While the wealthy Israelites made bread from wheat, poorer families used barley almost exclusively. For the poor, wheat flour was a luxury. As both the Northern and Southern Kingdoms aged, the separation between the wealthy who ate wheat bread and the poor who made bread from barley grew. Kings and leaders, insulated by their wealth, had almost no understanding of the everyday lives of the poor in their nations.

****

Ponder the relationship between national and individual sins.

1. Differentiate between national and personal sins. Can your nation sin and an individual not sin? Can an individual sin and her nation not you sin?

2. When we confess our sins, do we normally confess our individual sins or national sins?

3. How can we confess sins of our nation to God? What can we as individuals do about national sins?

****

The analogy for the farmer selecting varied methods to sow different types of seed, i.e., herbs versus grains, demonstrates that God's judgements aren't arbitrary. God doesn't stereotype his people. Carefully, he selects the judgement and discipline suited for a person's needs. God uses the lightest possible touch. He never allows his judgment to be greater than his people can bear. Israel's sins were so detestable that the nation was destroyed. In contrast God punished Judah for sins, but didn't punish them forever. The punishment had an endpoint. A glorious future awaited the redeemed nation. As a farmer doesn't plow a field forever, so Judah's punishment won't last forever.

****

God doesn't have set punishment for sin. God punishes each individual who sins according to his/her level of knowledge and abilities. Is that fair (just)?

****

Often Bible commentators compared Isaiah's parable of the plowman to Jesus's teachings in the New Testament. Several asserted that Jesus's parable of the wheat and tares echoed Isaiah's plowman parable. Others suggested that Jesus's teaching in Matthew 16:2-4 where the Pharisees and Sadducees couldn't interpret signs of the times had its origins in Isaiah's plowman parable. It makes sense that Jesus based his teachings and parable on Old Testament writings because the Holy Spirit—the third entity of the Trinity—gave the parables to Old Testament prophets and writers.

Final Thoughts:
Scripture tells us that we reap what we sow. How can taking the time to hear and learn about God and his statutes help us to sow more wisely?

Chapter 9
Vision of an Almond Branch

Getting Started: Read Jeremiah 1:11-12

Most Old Testament parables were heard; they stimulated the ear and appealed to the auditory sense. The almond branch parable was different. God gave it to Jeremiah in a vision. Because the parable was visual doesn't make it less important. As with most messages from God, Jeremiah's record began with "The word of the Lord."

Jeremiah was from the priestly family of Hilkiah. His home was the town Anathoth, a short three to four miles northeast of Jerusalem. Bible scholars believe God called Jeremiah to be a prophet when Jeremiah was as young as 12-13 years of age. By this point in history (about 627 BC), Assyria had conquered the Northern Kingdom (Israel). Many Israelites living there were exiled throughout the Assyrian Empire; however, some fled to Judah and Jerusalem. The military and political powers in the near East were Egypt southwest of Judah and Babylon to the east.

Shortly after God called Jeremiah to be his prophet, God gave Jeremiah two inaugural visions. The first encompassed an almond branch. The vision is sometimes regarded as part of God's training of Jeremiah to be a prophet. God expected Jeremiah to see and interpret the vision. Jeremiah was to use his senses and mind in service to God. Jeremiah had to participate in the explanation of God's message.

Good King Josiah (640-609 BC) was on Judah's throne; he initiated religious reforms to return Judah to worship of the true God. Jeremiah was a strong supporter of Josiah's actions. Unfortunately, after King Josiah's death, subsequent kings (Jehoahaz, Jehoiakim, Jehoiachin, and Zedekiah) abandoned Josiah's reforms. In 586 BC, Jerusalem was destroyed by the Babylonians; however, when God gave Jeremiah the almond branch parable, Jerusalem's destruction was 40-50 years in the future.

In this parable, God showed Jeremiah an almond branch. The vision was followed by questions and answers between God and Jeremiah. Jeremiah recorded:

> The word of the LORD came to me:
> 'What do you see, Jeremiah?'
> 'I see the branch of an almond tree,'
> I replied. The LORD said to me,
> 'You have seen correctly, for I am watching to see
> that my word is fulfilled' (Jeremiah 1:11-12).

My first reaction to this parable was, "What in the world? How does an almond tree relate to God watching to see that his word is fulfilled in the world?" Subsequent investigation showed that the Hebrew word for almond tree was *shâqêd*.[1] *Shâqêd* translates: to be alert, awake, sleepless, and on the lookout. For many centuries, even a millennium, the almond tree and blooms were symbols of watchfulness and wakefulness to the children of Israel.

****

Job called God "a watcher of men."

1. Read Job 7:20.

2. Clearly, Job thought that God was watching him. Do you think that God is watching you? Does the God of the universe watch you? Does he even have time to do that?

3. If God is watching my behavior, should I be doing anything different than what I am doing now? What would that be?

****

The almond tree is the first tree to bloom in the new year in Israel; it wakes up early. Generally, the almond tree starts to flower the middle of February; however, in the Negev Desert almond tree buds and blossoms are seen as early as January. Similar to the blooming of an almond tree, God recruited Jeremiah to be his prophet early in Jeremiah's life.

Israelites grew and harvested almonds from sweet almond trees. The almond tree grew about 30 feet high and was often used for shade for people and livestock. Almonds were pressed into almond oil and occasionally almonds were ground and made into flour. Similar to the multiple uses of an almond tree, God communicated with Jeremiah multiple ways over Jeremiah's approximately four decades as a prophet. Further, Jeremiah communicated God's message to the nation of Judah in multiple ways, i.e., speaking, writing, and action.

In the days of Jeremiah, both a male and a female flowering almond tree were needed for propagation. The need for a male and female almond tree to get an almond crop reminds me that in the disastrous years before the fall of Jerusalem, both men and women worshiped idols and turned from serving God. Neither husbands nor wives attempted to draw their spouses from idol worship to worship the living God.

In comparison to some other trees in the Promised Land, the almond tree is relatively short-lived. Young almond trees begin to produce almond crops in their third-or-fourth year of growth. Often Israelites cut almond trees down after 25 years; however, some almond trees are productive into old age, i.e., 50 years or more, just as Jeremiah continued to be God's prophet into his old age. A component of God's judgement on Judah, i.e., the Babylonian exile, was that it was relatively short-lived (70 years), similar to the productive life span of most almond trees.

Almond tree

Maria Lin

Almonds

When God gave Jeremiah the parable of the almond branch, he gave Jeremiah its interpretation. The interpretation was that God was watching and alert to see that his word was fulfilled in Judah. When Jeremiah saw the almond branch with its blooming flowers, possibly he interpreted the vision as a message of hope for Judah. Unfortunately, subsequent visions God gave to Jeremiah carried little hope for Judah's immediate future. Just as the almond tree was a sign of spring, it symbolized and heralded the judgment that God pronounced on Judah, i.e., through Joel, Isaiah, and Zephaniah. The ruinous spiritual condition of Judah's people meant God had to destroy Judah before he could rebuild the nation.[4]

****

As a child I visualized God watching me like an "all seeing eye."

Take a $1.00 bill out of your wallet and look on the back side. See the eye on the top of the pyramid.

1. The two Latin phrases on the $1.00 bill are "*Annuit Coeptis*" which means Providence Has Favored Our Undertakings and "*Novus Ordo Seclorum*" means A New Order of the Ages. How can both refer to God as a watcher?

2. My 90- year-old friend keeps a $1.00 in her nursing home room. She says the eye reminds her that God is watching her and that the triangular sides of the pyramid remind her of the Trinity. I like her interpretation better than the historical meaning of the Great Seal of the United States. What about you? Which meaning do you prefer?

****

In the Bible the almond tree was mentioned several places prior to Jeremiah's vision. When Jacob (approximately 1875 BC) directed his sons to go to Egypt to buy grain, he told them to take almonds as a gift to the Egyptian rulers. Several Bible historians contended that almonds were a delicacy only the very rich could afford; therefore, almonds were a valuable gift for an Egyptian pharaoh. Possibly, Joseph or the Israelites who settled Goshen introduced almond trees into Egypt.

Israelites knew the beauty and significance of almond trees. Almond tree buds and blossoms appeared on the Tabernacle lampstand (Exodus 25:33-34). Each of the six side branches and central branch was decorated with almond buds and flowers. Aaron's staff was made of almond wood. It was his staff that sprouted and produced almond buds, blossoms, and nuts when placed in front of the Ark of the Covenant overnight. In both instances – on the lampstand and on Aaron's rod – the almond symbolized the need for Israelites to watch that they obeyed God in all actions. By the time of Jeremiah, the nation of Judah forgot God's warning to citizens, priests, and rulers to watch their beliefs and actions.

In Ecclesiastes (12:5) almond tree blossoms are used politely to describe the white hair of aged men. Because Israelites valued old age, a comparison of an elderly man to a white almond tree blossom was a mark of respect. Male family elders were to be watchers so that godly traditions and relationships were maintained in the family.

Final Thoughts:
Remember, the childhood rhyme, "Stop, look, and listen before you cross the street. Use your eyes, use your ears, then use your feet."
How could the meaning of that rhyme apply to your Christian life?

Chapter 10
Two Baskets of Figs

Getting Started: Read Jeremiah chapter 24

Jeremiah's parable of two baskets of figs contrasted Judah captives taken to Babylon with those who remained in Jerusalem and Judah. The captives taken to Babylon were named "good;" while those who remained in Judah were identified as "bad." Rarely, in history are captives designated the "good guys;" but, if we have learned anything about God, it is that he turns our preconceived ideas of right-wrong, rich-poor, and good-bad upside down.

By the time of this parable, Jeremiah had been God's prophet for about 23 years. In the years prior to Jeremiah's parable of the two baskets of figs, Judah's King Jehoiakim was murdered. His son, Jehoiachin, succeeded his father to the throne. After ruling three months and ten days, the eighteen-year-old king surrendered when Nebuchadnezzar besieged Jerusalem. This grandson of godly King Josiah, his mother and wives, capable fighting men, and the most skilled artisans and craftsmen were taken captive (597 BC) to Babylon. Nebuchadnezzar made Jehoiachin's uncle, Zedekiah, the vassal king in Judah.

In the parable of the two baskets of figs, God gave Jeremiah a vision that included a parable:

> After Jehoiachin son of Jehoiakim king of Judah and the officials, the skilled workers and the artisans of Judah were carried into exile from Jerusalem to

Babylon by Nebuchadnezzar king of Babylon, the Lord showed me two baskets of figs placed in front of the temple of the Lord. One basket had very good figs, like those that ripen early; the other basket had very bad figs, so bad they could not be eaten (Jeremiah 24: 1-3 NIV)

The reader isn't sure if Jeremiah was at the front of the Jerusalem temple when he saw the two baskets of figs, or if he was elsewhere and God included both the temple and baskets of figs in the vision. Immediately, Jeremiah noticed that one basket of figs contained good figs, they looked succulent and edible. In contrast, the second basket of figs was bad. The Bible didn't specify how the second basket of figs looked. Perhaps, the figs were mushy, spoiled, or rotten; or, they could have been small and dry. Whatever was wrong with these figs, they couldn't be eaten.

Then the Lord asked me, What do you see, Jeremiah? Figs, I answered. The good ones are very good, but the bad ones are so bad they cannot be eaten (Jeremiah 24:3-4 NIV).

The question that God asked Jeremiah in this parable is the same one that he asked Jeremiah in the vision of the almond branch, "What do you see?" As with the first vision, God gave Jeremiah, God expected his prophet to not just look at, but to understand, the vision. Jeremiah's response was accurate, i.e., he saw a basket of good and a basket of inedible, bad figs. Then, God interpreted the vision of two baskets of figs to Jeremiah:

Then the word of the Lord came to me: This is what the Lord, the God of Israel, says: Like these good figs, I regard as good the exiles from Judah, whom I sent away
from this place to the land of the Babylonians. My eyes
will watch over them for their good, and I will bring them back to this land. I will build them up and not tear

them down; I will plant them and not uproot them. I will

give them a heart to know me, that I am the Lord. They

will be my people, and I will be their God, for they will

return to me with all their heart (Jeremiah 24:4-7 NIV).

****

God expected the captive Jews not to resent their captivity or captors.

1.   Describe how you would feel if you were uprooted from you home and taken captive into another country.

2.   How hard would it be for you to agree with God that you deserved exile as your punishment?

3.   How should refugees be treated by Christians in the country where they seek asylum?

****

Jeremiah's use of the word *then* at the start of this section could imply a time lapse between God giving the vision to Jeremiah and giving its interpretation. Perhaps in the interim, God wanted Jeremiah to reflect on the vision, use his intelligence, and figure out the parable's meaning. Clearly, God regarded the exiles taken captive to Babylon as good figs. He planned to watch over them during their captivity and bring them back to Judah. In addition, God will give the captives a heart to know him and they will turn to God with all their heart.

The balance of Chapter 24 is God's interpretation of the basket of bad figs:

But like the bad figs, which are so bad they cannot be eaten, says the Lord, so will I deal with Zedekiah king of Judah, his officials and the survivors from

Jerusalem, whether they remain in this land or live in Egypt. I will make them abhorrent and an offense to all the kingdoms of the earth, a reproach and a byword, a curse and an object of ridicule, wherever I banish them. I will send the sword, famine and plague against them until they are destroyed from the land I gave to them and their ancestors (Jeremiah 24:8-10 NIV).

In contrast to the good figs, the outcome for the bad figs was dire. The bad figs were King Zedekiah, his officials, and other survivors of the Babylonian siege of Jerusalem. God was going to send sword, famine, and plague on people who remained in Judah. Indeed, during the siege of Jerusalem, residents suffered famine and pestilence. When the Babylonians broke through the Jerusalem walls, soldiers murdered thousands of Jerusalemites. Survivors were exported to foreign kingdoms. God determined to make these exported Judahites abhorrent to the people of every kingdom where the Babylonians settled them.

****

Exile was the price the Jews paid for disobeying God
by worshiping idols and treating fellow Israelites with contempt.

1. Despite their rebellion against God, many Judahites continued to make sacrifices at God's temple. Today, we don't make burnt offerings to God. Instead we give money to the church and worthy charities. Are we mimicking the behavior of Judahites? Explain your answer.

2. What if most of our actions are godly, but inside we are angry and resentful? Is exhibiting godly behavior sufficient, or do we have to have a change in our heart? How can we change our hearts?

3. Samuel told the Israelites that to obey God is better than to make sacrifices to him? How would you apply Samuel's words to your life?

****

Several characteristics of fig trees and their fruit make them a good illustration for Jeremiah's vision of a good and bad baskets of figs. Although a relatively small tree, fig trees figured prominently in Israelite lore and holy writings. Supposedly, Adam and Eve used fig leaves to first clothe their bodies. The fig leaves in the Adam and Eve account symbolized their disobedience to God in much the same way that most of Judah's people disobeyed God's laws. Fig leaves are large (typically 5-10 inches long and 4-5 inches wide) and attractive, but, they are rough and hairy on the underside. When injured, leaves exude a bitter, sticky, and milky resin. Adam and Eve sowed several fig leaves together to create aprons to cover their naked bodies. These fig leaf clothes would have been itchy, sticky, and altogether uncomfortable against the skin. Judah's choices to disobey God and hide in their sin resulted in much more than mere discomfort.

Through Moses, God told the Israelites that the fig tree would be one of the seven species of plants that would enrich their lives in the Promised Land; yet, fig trees aren't exceptionally hardy. They grow best in a narrow environment. The average fig tree grows about twenty feet tall and develops a spreading canopy. The trunk is short; bark is gray and smooth. The tree trunk is sensitive to heat and sun and easily damaged. Further, fig trees can be damaged if temperatures drop to 30 degrees Fahrenheit. Perhaps, the bad figs in Jeremiah's parable came from a tree that received too much summer heat or were damaged by an early frost.

Sometimes figs grow under leaves and at other times above leaves. In the Middle East, fig trees bear fruit twice a year.[7] The winter (first) fig crop ripens in June; the summer (second) crop ripens August through September. Often on fig trees, fruit (figs) appears prior to, or with, leaves. Remember, during Passover, Jesus walked to a fig tree on his way from Bethany to Jerusalem (Mark 11:12-14). Because he saw leaves on the fig tree, Jesus expected the tree would contain figs he could eat. The fig tree contained leaves, but no figs. As with Jeremiah's basket of bad figs, Christ concluded, the fig tree was useless. The proper response was to cut down the useless tree (Luke 13:6-9).

Unique among flowering trees, fig flowers aren't seen; rather, flowers are enclosed inside the fig (fruit) itself. Similar to the hidden fig flower, God wanted Judahites to produce good works, not for outward display, but, to sweeten the lives of individuals around them. Unfortunately, the last four kings of Judah evidenced little, if any, good fruit in their lives. Individual citizens of Judah followed the lead of their kings.

After four years of growth, most fig trees begin to produce fruit. Ideally, figs ripen fully before they are picked. A fig is ripe when it darkens, turns brown or purple, starts to bend at the neck, and is slightly soft to the touch. Because all figs don't ripen at the same time, harvest occurs over several months. To get the basket of bad figs, Judahites may have picked all of the figs at the same time. They didn't realize or care that some figs weren't ripe and wouldn't ripen off the tree branch.

Good Figs   Bad Figs

Alicia Lin

Jeremiah's prophecy of the good and bad figs came true. When Jehoiachin arrived in Babylon, he was placed in prison. There, he remained 37 years. When Nebuchadnezzar died, his son Evil-Murdock became king over Babylon. King Evil-Murdock released

Jehoiachin from prison, gave him an allowance, and a favored place at the king's high table for meals. Seventy years after Jehoiachin's captivity, his grandson, Zerubbabel, led the first 50,000 Jews who left Babylon and returned to Jerusalem. God considered the exiled Jews as good figs.

****

I cried out, "Just tell me what you want me to learn from this situation so I can get past the mental pain."

1.   A number of years ago, I had a big professional disappointment and was mentally hurt. Why do we have to experience mental pain?

2.   Physically, pain is a symptom that something is wrong in the body. If you had to ponder mental pain in your own life, is symptom? Explain your answer.

3.   In retrospect, I am sure that God wanted me to experience the pain, so I would rely more on him and could empathize with other's pain and loss. Have you ever had such an experience? How did you react?

****

Meanwhile back in Jerusalem, King Zedekiah rebelled against Babylon. Nebuchadnezzar returned to Jerusalem, laid siege to the city, killed King Zedekiah, and conquered Jerusalem and the surrounding towns. Nebuchadnezzar assigned Gedaliah, a politically moderate Jew, as governor of Judea. Governor Gedaliah established his capital at Mizpah.

Ishmael, a member of Judah's former royal family, killed Gedaliah and the Babylonian soldiers with him. The remaining Jews knew that Nebuchadnezzar would be furious at Governor Gedaliah's murder. They fled to Egypt for safety. Not too many years later, Nebuchadnezzar invaded Egypt. During the invasion his army killed most of the Jews who fled there. Thus, the bad figs were destroyed.

Final Thoughts:
Most American resonate to New Hampshire's state motto, "Live free or die." Yet, God told the Jewish exiles to do the opposite, i.e., submit to and live under the yoke of Babylonian oppressors.

Chapter 11
Parable of Famine Bread

Getting Started: Read Ezekiel chapter 4

At times, God instructed prophets to act out parables. About one-third of Ezekiel's parables were action parables. Some, but not all, were accompanied by words. In chapter 4 Ezekiel recorded how he acted out three parables—he uttered no words. Jews in Babylon had to interpret Ezekiel's actions. All three parables depicted the severity of the coming siege of Jerusalem.

Ezekiel was both a prophet and priest. He was taken to Babylon when King Nebuchadnezzar took Judah's King Jehoiachin and 10,000 captives from Jerusalem to Babylon (597 BC). At that time, Nebuchadnezzar established Zedekiah as puppet king over Judah. Although a captive, Ezekiel lived in his own house near the Chebar River. God called Ezekiel as a prophet after he was exiled to Babylon. Ezekiel was a stern man, very aware of his divine commission. Frequently, Ezekiel referred to the Jews as "a rebellious house."

In Jerusalem, King Zedekiah rebelled against Nebuchadnezzar after ruling five-to-six year. King Zedekiah ceased paying tribute to Babylon and asked Egypt for military assistance to throw off Babylonian rule. Subsequently, Nebuchadnezzar laid siege to Jerusalem. After about 18 months, the Babylonian army breached the wall around Jerusalem.

When Nebuchadnezzar and his army started for Judah, Jerusalem was flooded with refugees fleeing the countryside. The influx was so great that private homes, inns, and the temple courtyard were crammed with people. The poor set up tents in the streets or lay down at night wherever they found an empty space. People and noise were everywhere; smoke billowed from cooking fires.

Although the situation was dire, it got worse after the Babylonians arrived and surrounded the city. No additional food supplies entered Jerusalem. Human and animal refuse couldn't be removed. Filth and stench were everywhere. Often dead bodies remained where individuals died, contributing to the stench and disease. Many people inside Jerusalem starved to death or died from disease. Some mothers killed and ate their children for food.

****

Can malnutrition, starvation, and famine be nonphysical?

1. Define malnutrition, starvation, and famine. You may want to look up each word in a dictionary.

> a. Malnourished
> b. Starvation
> c. Famine

2. How does each word (i.e., malnutrition, starvation, famine) impact the others?

3. If you were starving and had only human excrement to cook your food over, would it make a difference to you as you ate the food? Why did it matter to Ezekiel?

****

In Babylon, God instructed Ezekiel to act out the siege of Jerusalem. The first action parable used a clay tablet to depict the siege. The second had Ezekiel lying on his left side, followed by lying on his right side. The third parable encompassed plants. God told Ezekiel to use grains and legumes to prepare a loaf of bread:

Take wheat and barley, beans and lentils, millet and spelt; put them in a storage jar and use them to make bread for yourself" Weigh out twenty shekels of food to eat each day and eat it at set times. Also measure out a sixth of a hin of water and drink it at set times (Ezekiel 4:9-11 NIV).

Jewish dietary laws required Jews to make bread from only one type of flour, i.e., wheat, barley, millet, or spelt. Combining different flour sources in one vessel (container, bowl) was a desecration and contradicted Jewish dietary laws. Normally, legumes weren't used to make bread; however, extremely poor individuals used beans and occasionally lentils for bread flour. Mixing flour from several sources showed the scarcity of flour during the siege of Jerusalem.

Although bread from these flours was highly nutritious, the amount was below subsistence level. Ezekiel ate 20 shekels of bread daily or about eight-ten ounces (700-1100 calories). Oil added more calories to the bread mix. A sixth of a hin of water is about one and one-half pint or three eight-ounce cups. This amount of bread and water allowed Ezekiel to barely survive. God told Ezekiel that food and water would be so scarce in Jerusalem by the time the siege ended that people would be appalled when they saw ravages of famine on each other (Ezekiel 4:17).

The next three verses were a conversation between God and Ezekiel about how the bread should be prepared (Ezekiel 4:12-15). Initially, God told Ezekiel to bake his bread over human dung. When Ezekiel objected, God allowed him to bake his bread over cow manure; however, during the Babylonian siege of Jerusalem, Jews didn't have the luxury of using animal dung for baking. Near the end of the siege, no animals were alive in the city. All had been slaughtered for food. No wood was left. Human excrement was the primary cooking fuel.

God ends Ezekiel's action parables by interpreting them. God said to Ezekiel: "Son of man, I will cut off the supply of food in Jerusalem. The people will eat rationed food in anxiety and drink rationed water in despair" (Ezekiel 4:9-16 NIV).

The parables of the siege of Jerusalem were about coming judgment on Jerusalem. The people of Judah sinned so long and to such a degree that God removed his protection from around Jerusalem. When Ezekiel acted out the parables of the siege of Jerusalem, God still dwelled in the Jerusalem temple; however, before the Babylonians surrounded Jerusalem, God's presence left both the temple and Jerusalem (Ezekiel chapters 10 and 11). Importantly, Ezekiel's actions shouldn't be interpreted as sympathetic magic where something done to a model or person has a similar act in reality. True, Ezekiel making famine bread foreshadowed the starvation of the Jerusalemites; but, God caused the famine, not Ezekiel's behavior or magic.

****

How were God's absence from the Temple and the Babylonian sacking of Jerusalem and destruction of the Temple related?

1. Do you think that famine would have come to Jerusalem or Jerusalem would have been sacked by the Babylonians if God's presence remained in the temple? As you ponder your answer, read and summarize these three Bible references say:

    a. 2 Kings 16:1-5
    b. 2 Kings chapter 19
    c. 2 Kings 22 and 23:1-27. (Be sure to read the last two verses, i.e., 2 Kings 23:26-27).
    ****

The book of Ezekiel is one of the most detailed and well-known references to grains in the Bible; but, we also learn, or relearn, that Israelites dried and ground legumes (bean and lentils) into bread flour. For a plant in this parable, I describe the bean. In ancient Israel, beans were planted in late fall and matured in the spring. Bean plants are hearty enough to live through mild frosts. Young bean pods are green, three-to-six inches long, and contain two-to-six seeds called beans. Pods lower on the stalk mature first, while pods nearer the top mature later. If harvesting is delayed until all pods are ripe, pods nearer the plant bottom split and beans are lost. I wonder if fewer Jews would have died, or been killed, if God initiated judgment on Jerusalem sooner than he did.

Broad bean

Maria Lin

Despite our predisposition to consume meat, the multi-grain and legume bread that God told Ezekiel to eat likely provided a complete protein meal. Meat protein is composed of amino acids, nine of which are essential. Grains and legumes contain amino acids, but none contain all the essential amino acids. However, what one type of grain or legume lacked, another contained. Made from grain and legumes, likely Ezekiel's bread contain the complete set of essential amino acids. If eaten in sufficient quantity, this multigrain, multi-legume bread could have kept Ezekiel nourished. For the Jerusalemites, the challenge was having sufficient bread and calories to maintain life.

By combining bean and grain flour, God reminded Jerusalemites that they were more concerned about breaking relative minor dietary laws than with breaking the first commandment, i.e., "you shall have no other gods before me" (Exodus 20:3 NIV). In comparison to breaking the first commandment, combining grain and legume flour was a minor infraction. Equally, minor and relatively unimportant was the source of heat to bake the bread, i.e., use of human excrement rather than wood or animal dung.

The Babylonians laid siege to Jerusalem in 588/589 BC. About 18 months later the Jerusalem walls were breached. Nebuchadnezzar had no more patience with the rebellious Jews or his puppet king, Zedekiah. He had Zedekiah killed and the Jerusalem temple and major buildings destroyed. The wall around Jerusalem was razed. Many Jews not killed by famine and plague were killed by the Babylonian soldiers. Only the poorest Jews were allowed to remain in Judah.

****

If the Holy Spirit left you, what would your life be like?

1. Would you feel there was someone/something missing inside of you? Explain your feelings.

2. Do you think you would know cognitively (mentally) that someone/something missing in your life? Explain your feelings.

3. How do you think your behavior (actions) would change, or not change, as a result of the absence of the Holy Spirit?

****

Final Thoughts:
"The day is coming when I will send a
famine through the land—not a famine of
food or a thirst for water, but a famine for
the words of the Lord (Amos 8:11 NIV).

Chapter 12
Talking among Myrtle Trees

Getting Started: Read Zechariah 1:8-13

The parable of the man among the myrtle trees was a prophetic vision, designed to appeal to the eyes rather than the ears. Jews regarded the myrtle as a symbol of something good and beautiful; yet, the myrtle tree couldn't compare to the cedar of Lebanon. The parable was set in Judea, an insignificant province of the Persian Empire.

The first year (535-536 BC) the Jews returned to Jerusalem from Babylonian they rebuilt the temple altar. The second year, they laid the second temple's foundation. Non-Jewish people who lived in the area, largely Samaritans, offered to help rebuild the temple. When the Jews refused their assistance, these enemies initiated a systematic program to discourage the Jew's efforts. As a result temple construction slowed, then, stopped for about 10 years.

In August 520 BC, God spoke through the Jewish prophet Haggai. God told the Jews to finish building the temple. Haggai identified that the drought in Judea was the result of God's temple remaining in ruins. Although returned Jews built their own homes, they didn't rebuild God's home. Almost immediately, Jews reinitiated temple construction.

Two months after God's message to Haggai, Zechariah started to receive messages from God. Zechariah's prophecies mirrored Haggai's, i.e., rebuild the temple; but, included that the Jews repent and serve the Lord. Zechariah was God's prophet for the next 40 years (520-480 BC).

In the first year of his ministry, Zechariah received eight visions from God in one night. They were visions, not dreams; Zechariah was fully awake. The first vision was a parable that included a plant, the myrtle tree. Here is Zechariah first vision:

> There before me was a man mounted on a red horse. He was standing among the myrtle trees in a ravine. Behind him were red, brown and white horses. I asked, "What are these, my lord?"
>
> The angel who was talking with me answered, 'I will show you what they are.'
>
> Then the man standing among the myrtle trees explained, 'They are the ones the Lord has sent to go throughout the earth. And they reported to the angel of the Lord who was standing among the myrtle trees, We have gone throughout the earth and found the whole world at rest and in peace.'
>
> Then the angel of the Lord said, "Lord Almighty, how long will you withhold mercy from Jerusalem and from the towns of Judah, which you have been angry with these seventy years?"
>
> So the Lord spoke kind and comforting words to the angel who talked with me.
>
> Then the angel who was speaking to me said, 'Proclaim this word: This is what the Lord Almighty says: I am very jealous for Jerusalem and Zion, and I am very angry with the nations that feel secure. I was only a little angry, but they went too far with the punishment. Therefore this is what the Lord says: I will return to Jerusalem with mercy, and there my house will be rebuilt. And the measuring line will be stretched out over Jerusalem, declares the Lord

Almighty. Proclaim further: This is what the Lord Almighty says: My towns will again overflow with prosperity, and the Lord will again comfort Zion and choose Jerusalem' (Zechariah 1:8-17 NIV).

Prophets were God's voice on earth. They spoke or recorded exactly what God said, rather than paraphrasing or interpreting God's message. When we examine the details of the parable, we see two conversations. One conversation is between Zechariah and an angel. The second conversation is between "the angel of the Lord" (pre-incarnate Jesus) and God. The parable's setting is a ravine and the tree is a myrtle.

****

If you were a postexile Jew living in Jerusalem, how would you respond to Zechariah's parable of the man among the myrtle trees?

1. Would you have been encouraged or discouraged by Zechariah' parable? Explain your reasoning.

2. Would there have been any part of you that wondered how God could allow Babylon to enact such vicious brutality on the people of Jerusalem? Possibly, Jerusalemites that lived through the siege and the sacking of Jerusalem saw beloved parents or grandparents die or be murdered.

3. Would you have been a) angry with God, b) grateful that God cared about you and your people enough to discipline you, or c) totally confused about God's supposed goodness?

****

At the time of Zechariah's prophecy, myrtle trees grew wild throughout Judea. The myrtle is an evergreen shrub or small tree, i.e., under optimal conditions myrtle trees grow up to 24 feet. The myrtle tree grew under the canopy of taller trees or where taller trees were harvested or destroyed. Using the myrtle tree to symbolize Jews, represented that both in the present and in the future, Jews were a small nation. No longer was the Jewish nation comparable to the 120-foot cedar of Lebanon.

The myrtle leaf is dark green, oval, and pointed. Leaves are fragrant because the leaf tissue contains oil-secreting glands. Myrtle leaves and flowers have attractive scents which are often described as sweet, flower-like, aromatic, and unique. Like a leaf from the insignificant myrtle tree, Jews could still give off a sweet odor pleasing to God.

In Zechariah's parable, myrtle trees grew in a ravine. A ravine is a narrow steep-sided valley, a low place. Myrtle trees don't tolerate shade; yet, shade is a common characteristic of a ravine or gorge. Further, myrtle trees are damaged by cold dry wind and when young are damaged by frost. In a ravine—the microclimate and setting of Zechariah's parable—young myrtle trees could be damaged by shade, cold, and wind blowing through the ravine. Similarly, the Jewish remnant in Judea could be easily damaged, even destroyed, by conquerors. Future Jewish nations could thrive, but only in the shadow of mighty nations.

The Hebrew word for myrtle tree is *hădaç*.[1] Little is known about the derivation of *hădaç*; however, it may mean "to grow rapidly." In contrast, the word for cedar is *'erez*[1] meaning "to be firm." Firm means securely or solidly fixed in place and having a structure that resists pressure. The cedar tree was firm because of its tenacious root structure, long life in nature, resistance to insect infestation, and endurance as a building material (see additional characteristics of the cedar tree under The Cedar and Thistle).

****

Advantages of being a myrtle tree??????

Identify some advantages of being a myrtle rather than a cedar tree.

1.

2.

3.

****

Myrtle

Maria Lin

Like the fast-growing myrtle tree, the population in postexile Judea grew rapidly. Some population increase was due to birth rates; but, more probably, Jewish population increased because Jews moved into Judea from other parts of the Persian Empire. With God's assistance the Jews grew again into a nation; however, like the myrtle tree, the Jews didn't have the national durability and firmness seen in King David and Solomon's reigns. The once mighty cedar of Lebanon was gone; it was now a somewhat lowly myrtle tree. Judea was a small province in the outback of the expansive Persian Empire. Going forward, most of Judean history showed that the country was controlled by foreign nations, i.e., Rome, Turkey, Great Britain.

Despite the diminished importance of the Jewish kingdom, Zechariah's parable was a message of hope and encouragement to postexile Jews. The interpretation was that God keeps his promises. God comforted the angel who was distressed about the state of the lives of the postexile Jews. God promised that the Babylonian-Persian Empire would be held accountable for their brutal treatment of his people when Judah and Jerusalem were conquered. Further, God promised that he would return to Jerusalem and Zion with mercy and the temple would be rebuilt.

****

God promised Jews in the tiny Judean province would prosper.

1. The Bible revealed some reasons why people prosper and reasons why they don't prosper in the following verses. Read and summarize reasons for prosperity from these Bible verses:

     a. Deuteronomy 28:62-63
     b. Proverbs 17:20
     c. Proverbs 28:13

2. How can we meld our personal experiences with what the Bible says, yes ,even promises, about prosperity being related to a godly life?

3. According to God's word, why have you prospered or not prospered?

****

Persian Emperor Darius III died about 330 BC, leaving Alexander of Greece ruler of much of the remaining lands of the once mighty Persian Empire. About 200 years had passed between God consoling the angel of the Lord and God holding the Babylonian-Persian Empire accountable for their brutal treatment of the Jerusalem Jews. Within those 200 years Persia fought and lost many battles with vicious enemies where soldiers and civilians were ruthlessly killed.

We are reminded anew that God keeps his promises, but, God doesn't operate within the same time constraints as man.

Final Thoughts:
Does God need to return to the United States of America in a way similar to his promise to return to Jerusalem? If so, what is your role in making this happen?

Section 2
Plants in New Testament Parables

In contrast to the few books written on Old Testament parables, there is an overabundance on New Testament parables. Almost New Testament parable books focus on Jesus's parables; however, other New Testament figures told parables, i.e., John the Baptist, Paul, James, Peter, and John the Apostle. Many of these writers used plants to illustrate their spiritual message. Section 2, Plants in New Testament Parables, contains twelve parables in the New Testament illustrated by plants. Seven parables were given by Jesus and five by other New Testament figures.

The New Testament was written in Greek; the Greek word *parabŏlē* was used for parable.[1] *Parabŏlē* translates as a comparison, placing beside, and fictitious narrative usually of common life conveying moral truth. Some New Testament truths were comparisons and illustrations presented as simple stories. Others were acted out or seen in visions.

Parable development reached its zenith in Jesus's parables; about 1/3 of his words were parables. But, Jesus didn't start his ministry telling parables. Think back to Jesus's Sermon on the Mount. Despite covering several chapters (Matthew 5-7), the Sermon contains few parables. Imagine the disciple's surprise when one day Jesus's teaching method changed. He started to teach almost exclusively in parables. The disciples were as confused as the crowds who came to hear Jesus. They asked Jesus why he was using parables.

Jesus's used parables for three reasons. First, parables prevented the Jewish leaders—many who were or would become Jesus's enemies—from using his own words to condemn him. Second, Jesus's use of parables fulfilled Isaiah's prophecy that people wouldn't understand, when even the Messiah spoke, because they were spiritually dull (Isaiah 6:9-10). Third, parables contained truths that could only be understood through God's revelation. Although God wanted all individuals to understand the parables, the sad truth was some wouldn't understand because they weren't willing to accept Jesus and his message. But, to those individuals who were willing to accept Jesus as Messiah, interpretation of parables provided insight into the kingdom of God.

Jesus teachings never seem outdated. Jesus's parables are as relevant as "alerts" that flash on FOX or CNN news networks. Jesus spoke seven parables in Section 2, but they aren't an exhaustive list of Jesus's parables. They are included because they were the foundation of what Jesus wanted people to know about the kingdom of heaven and because they don't repeat any plant already described in Section 1, Plants in Old Testament Parables.

Jesus and John the Baptist lived and taught in Galilee, Judea, and in the trans-Jordan area known as Perea. Collectively, these areas are called the Holy Lands. Logically, both thought of plants in their own country when they included plants in parables. Other New Testament parable givers, i.e., Paul, the author of Hebrews, Peter, and John (who authored Revelations), probably wrote from other parts of Asia Minor or southeastern Europe. Nevertheless, Hebrew scholars and botanists consistently identified Holy Land plants when naming plants used to illustrate these parables.

Chapter 13
John the Baptist and Winnowing Wheat

Getting Started: Read Matthew 3:12

John the Baptist spoke a parable to foretell actions of the coming Messiah (Christ). John used the familiar agricultural metaphor of separating (winnowing) good grains of wheat from useless chaff. John taught that when Christ comes, he would separate Godly believers from those with a superficial or no belief in God. John's parable is about destiny.

In the early part of the first century, residents of Judea and Galilee were fairly prosperous. No wars ravaged these regions which were part of the Roman Empire. Most residents knew how to work within the Roman political and economic systems. The sentiment "just keep things level," reflected the self-interest and expediency of residents.

****

Lessons from hummingbirds.

Bruce and I stayed for a long weekend at a small resort in Canada called Destiny Bay. Over long dinners, we watched hummingbirds frenetically fly from one feeder to another, drinking the nectar.

1. The hummingbirds were so busy that they never slowed down to think about their destiny. Is their behavior in any way a reflection of yours? Explain your answer.

2. Think about standing before the judgement seat of God. How do you think you will feel?

3. What are you going to say when God asks you to give an account of your behavior here on earth?

****

A prophet, John the Baptist was born to Zechariah and Elizabeth. His hometown was in the hill country of Judea. Zechariah was from the family of Abijah, a division of priests that rotated to Jerusalem to burn daily incense in the temple. Realistically, John followed in Zechariah's footsteps and became the village priest. As a member of Abijah's priestly family, John probably had at least one rotation in the Jerusalem temple prior to his sojourn in the wilderness.

John preached personal acknowledgement and repentance of sins followed by baptism—full body emersion—in water as an outward sign of repentance. The baptismal water symbolically washed sins away. Some Jews recalled the words of the prophets about a coming Messiah. Many yearned for the Messiah's arrival. When these people heard about John and saw his actions, they asked John if he was the predicted savior. John answered their question with a firm denial saying that the coming Messiah was mightier than he (Matthew 3:11). John wasn't worthy to take off or carry the sandals of the Messiah. John went on to say that the Messiah will baptize people with the Holy Spirit and with fire.

John didn't stop with his message of repentance and physical act of baptism. John exhorted those baptized to change their behavior and bear fruit consistence with repentance (Luke 3:8-14). When those baptized asked him what they should do, John's answer wasn't that they quit their jobs; rather, in their lives and jobs, they should act honorably, treat others fairly, and share with the less fortunate. For example, John told men with two tunics to give one to the man who had none. Soldiers should stop accusing people falsely and extorting money from them.

John the Baptist spoke bluntly to the multitudes that came to him for baptism; but reserved his worst denunciations for Jerusalem's elite, i.e., Pharisees, Sadducees, and priests. He called them "vipers" (Luke 3:7). The fierceness of his words suggests firsthand knowledge of their behavior. Perhaps, when he rotated through the

Jerusalem temple as a priest, John saw the excesses, insincerity, and, yes, even corruption that infected priests of the Herodian-style Jerusalem temple.

****

Is anyone above the need to repent?

1. Do you think the elite, upper-crust Pharisees, Sadducees, and wealthy Jerusalemites in first century Palestine believed that a country priest/prophet's words applied to them? Why or why not?

2. Why did John label these men as "vipers?"

3. How would you compare most of today's intelligent and talented politicians and pundits to the Pharisees, Sadducees, and Jerusalem leaders who came to see John?

****

John the Baptist spoke several parables that used plants to make the comparison between the physical reality and spiritual truth, i.e., "the axe is laid to the root of the trees Every tree therefore that does not bear good fruit is cut down and will be thrown into the fire" (Luke 3:9 NIV). His parable on winnowing described separating chaff from wheat kernels:

> His winnowing fan (shovel, fork) is in His hand, and
> He will thoroughly clear out and clean His threshing
> floor and gather and store His wheat in His barn, but
> the chaff He will burn up with fire that cannot be put
> out (Matthew 3:12 AMP).

In ancient Judea, wheat kernels (seed, grain) were separated from the chaff (stalks, straw) on threshing floors. Generally, chaff was unusable except as fodder for livestock. The farmer separated wheat kernels from chaff using a process called winnowing. Winnowing consisted of throwing the threshed material (chaff and grain) into the air with a fork or a flat basket. The wind separated the valuable grains of wheat from the chaff. Because wheat kernels were heavier than chaff, they fell to the ground or back into the basket. The lighter chaff, dirt, etc., were blown away by the wind. At times, farmers used fans to create air currents to blow chaff and other impurities away from valuable wheat kernels.

Through most Old Testament time, poor Israelites used barley for bread. By the New Testament era, wheat was used for bread, other baking, and cereal. Ancient peoples called wheat the "giving grain" and associated it with the cycle of birth, life, and death. For the ancient Hebrews, wheat symbolized life from God, primarily physical life. For New Testament era people, John could have identified no better plant than wheat to contrast righteous and unrighteous individuals.

From earliest times, man planted wheat because of its high nutritional—life giving—content. Like barley, wheat was an annual crop; however wheat required a longer growing season (about 100 days) than barley. Usually, wheat was harvested in May. The longer growing season for wheat than for barley could have reassured John's listeners. John acknowledged that repentance, maturation, and amendment of life take time just as wheat took time to grow. The Presence Bread for the Tabernacle and Temple was made with fine white wheat flour. God had every right to expect that Jew's actions, especially those of Jewish leaders, were pure similar to the purist wheat flour used in Tabernacle bread.

John the Baptist spoke his parable on winnowing wheat soon after starting his ministry. Yet, John's parable demonstrated a sure knowledge of a different outcome for the righteous versus the unrighteous. Perhaps, John the Baptist's words on winnowing, wheat, and chaff had their origins in Psalm 1:4-5, i.e., the wicked are like chaff that the wind blows away. They won't be able to stand when God judges them. Sinners will be separated from the assembly of the righteous as chaff is separated from wheat kernels.

Winnowing Wheat   Maria Lin

****

When Christ is done, the threshing floor will be empty.
1. Given John's parable, what is going to happen to men and women who are on the fence, who haven't decided to follow Jesus?

2. Is there going to be an opportunity for a "do over" when Jesus comes the second time? Explain your position using verses from the Bible.

3. What will be your destiny when Jesus separates wheat from chaff?

****

When John the Baptist told the parable of winnowing wheat and chaff, the spiritual reality was that the coming Messiah (Christ) would distinguish or separate the righteous from the unrighteous. Jesus would critically analyze people's heart, not pious actions. John said that sincere, righteous individuals—wheat kernels—will be taken and stored in the farmer's barn, i.e., heaven. In contrast, chaff, those with pretend piety, will be forever burned.

Final Thoughts:
God isn't going to accept any dirt, chaff, or stray into his barn. Where does that leave you?

Chapter 14
Harvesting Weeds (Darnel)

Getting Started: Read Matthew 13:24-30, 36-43

The parable points toward the perplexing presence of evil on the earth by using a series of contrasts, i.e., the good farmer-enemy, wheat-tares, and two harvests. The parable was relevant to first century farmers because it described a common occurrence, i.e., wheat and weeds growing in the same field. Simultaneously, the parable was prophetic; it described what will happen at God's final harvest.

****

Many parables focus on a final outcome or eternity.

1. Why all these Bible writings, even warnings, allocated a final outcome for individuals? What so important about the final outcome?

2. Do you ever look at celebrities, whether politicians, actors, or pundits, and think that they are attractive and articulate? Do you envy them? Do you ever wonder what their relationship is with God? I've come to believe that I need to pray for, not envy, many of these celebrities.

3. Is silence consent? Are we silent about certain social issues because our lives haven't been fertilized enough?

****

Matthew is the only gospel writer who included Jesus's parable of the weeds. Because Matthew wrote for a primary Jewish audience, Jews were meant to interpret and apply the parable's content to their lives. Today, Christians can use the parable of the weeds to more fully understand God's actions on earth.

Chapter 14 begins with Jesus leaving a home where he was staying and taking a seat near the shore of the Sea of Galilee. In ancient times teachers sat when they taught, rather than standing behind a podium. Tradition locates Jesus's discourse at the "Cove of the Parables," a horseshoe-shaped amphitheater where Jesus's voice could carried to a crowd of hundreds (Matthew 13:1-2). Because Jesus was teaching in a rural area in Galilee, his audience knew about farming practices to include the damage that weeds do to wheat crops.

Likely, Jesus offered the parable of the weeds late in his first year, but more probably, early in his second year of public ministry. By this time scribes and Pharisees started to push back at him. They wanted Jesus to explain his "supposed" authority to teach and to give them a sign to verify his Messianic identity. Initially, Jesus spoke the parable of the wheat and weeds to a crowd. Later, he interpreted it for his disciples, but he never interpreted it for the crowds of people who came to listen to his teachings. Here is Christ's parable of the weeds:

> The kingdom of heaven may be compared to a man who sowed good seed in his field, but while his men were sleeping, his enemy came and sowed weeds among the wheat and went away. So when the plants came up and bore grain, then the weeds appeared also. And the servants of the master of the house came and said to him, 'Master, did you not sow good seed in your field? How then does it have weeds?'
>
> He said to them, 'An enemy has done this.'
>
> So the servants said to him, 'Then do you want us to go and gather them?'

But he said, 'No, lest in gathering the weeds you root up the wheat along with them. Let both grow together until the harvest, and at harvest time I will tell the reapers, Gather the weeds first and bind them in bundles to be burned, but gather the wheat into my barn'" (Matthew 13:24-30 ESV).

In the parable of the weeds, the weed was most likely darnel, also known as tares and poison ryegrass. Darnel originated in the Mediterranean region including the Middle East. Darnel is distributed widely throughout Israel to include extreme deserts. Like wheat, darnel is an annual plant; it grows in two-to-three-foot spikes. Again, like wheat, darnel spikes terminate in a grain head; however, the darnel grain head is longer than that of the wheat head and darnel lacks the fuzzy appearance of a wheat head. Initially, the darnel plant—stems, leaves and flowers—is green and looks like wheat.

When wheat and darnel are less developed, most farmers can't tell the difference between the two; however, as summer progresses, darnel plants turn black. The black color is a way to differentiate darnel from wheat which is creamy brown. Further, when both wheat and darnel are fully mature wheat stalks are taller than darnel.

Even a few grains of darnel negatively impact wheat crop quality. Darnel seeds are poisonous to people and livestock. Because darnel seeds are similar in appearance, size, and weight to wheat, it is difficult to separate or remove darnel seeds from wheat seeds. Often darnel seeds are contaminated with a variety of crop pests and diseases such as fungus. The best form of invasive species management is prevention, i.e., a farmer plants clean, wheat seeds. Recently developed herbicides kill darnel; however, in ancient Israelite farmers had no herbicides. They relied on sowing clean seeds to get a clean wheat crop.

Darnel

Wheat

The dialogue between the farmer and his servants showed the farmer's knowledge of both wheat and darnel seeds and growth patterns of both. Probably, the farmer didn't purchase wheat seed for planting; bought wheat seeds could be contaminated with darnel. Instead, the farmer used last year's wheat seed from his own fields. He and his servants knew that the wheat seeds they planted didn't contain darnel seeds. The only way fields could be contaminated with darnel was if the darnel seeds were deliberately planted.

When I first read that an enemy contaminated a farmer's wheat fields with weeds, I had a hard time believing the farmer's assertion that an enemy sowed weed in his field. The farmer sounded like he was making an excuse for careless planting of his fields. After investigating agriculture practices in first century Israel, I learned that jealous farmers often contaminated rivals' fields to discredit a rival farmer and to increase the value of wheat from their own fields.

****

Plant fertilizer contributes to plant growth and optimal fruit production.

1.   Name some bad fruit (sins) that we produce in our lives. If you need help, read Galatians 5:19-21.

2.   What does the Bible consider good fruit production in our lives? If you need help with this list, read Galatians 5:22-23.

3.   For plants, i.e., wheat, grapes, even weeds, to grow optimally, the soil conditions have to be right. Routinely, gardeners fertilize soil where plants grow. In contrast, often we neglect to fertilize the soil of our lives. What could or should we do to fertilize our walk with Christ?

****

Several verses after Jesus told the parable of the weeds, he provided its interpretation to disciples. Here is Jesus's explanation of the parable:

> The one who sows the good seed is the Son of Man. The field is the world, and the good seed is the sons of the kingdom. The weeds are the sons of the evil one, and the enemy who sowed them is the devil. The harvest is the end of the age, and the reapers are angels. Just as the weeds are gathered and burned with fire, so will it be at the end of the age. The Son of Man will send his angels, and they will gather out of his kingdom all causes of sin and all law-breakers, and throw them into the fiery furnace. In that place there will be weeping and gnashing of teeth. Then the righteous will shine like the sun in the kingdom of their Father (Matthew 13:35-43 NIV).

Jesus affirmed John the Baptist's parable of winnowed wheat when he told the disciples that at the final judgement wheat and weeds would be separated, i.e., the righteous placed in the barn or storehouse of God and the unrighteous thrown into a fiery furnace. Repeatedly, scripture writers affirmed that the course of human history is set toward judgement. No human will escape a judgment.

Jesus described how weeds came into the world and why they were allowed to grow. The origin of weeds on earth was Satan who sowed them in the pristine fields that God created. Remember, Satan sowed disobedience to God back in the Garden of Eden. Because God doesn't want anyone—any man or woman—to end up in the fiery furnace, he restrains his angels. They aren't allowed to pull out unrighteous, evil doers, until they mature. When it is abundantly clear that weeds are indeed weeds and not good wheat, angels reap or remove them, not to be placed in the storehouse of the Lord, but to be destroyed.

****

You have forsaken your first love" (Revelation 2:3-4 NIV).

1. What should be a Christian's first love?

2. How should we make amendment for forgetting our first love? If you aren't sure, read Revelation 2:5.

3. If you repent, amend your life, and return to your first love, what will Christ do for you (Revelation 2:7)?

****

In Revelation, John described a vision of the earth being harvested (Revelation 14:14-20). Grapes rather than weeds were harvested; however, the vision mirrors Jesus's parable of the weeds. Angels harvest grapes and throw them into the great winepress of God's wrath. The grapes were trampled and blood flowed outside the press. In this vision, John noted that the winepress was located outside the city. At the final harvest, evildoers aren't in the city wall or in God's barn (storehouse). In contrast, individuals who die in the Lord, i.e., they have a personal relationship with Christ, are blessed because their righteous deeds follow them into eternity (Revelation 13:13).

Final Thoughts:
In my home garden, weeds keep growing back even though I pull them out. My husband tells me to spray them with weed killer which is designed to kill roods. I'm reluctant to do that because the weed roots are so intertwined with the weed roots.

Chapter 15
Lily of the Field

Getting Started: Read Matthew 6:28-30

Jesus's parable of lilies adorning field grass is part of the Sermon on the Mount. Often considered Jesus inaugural address, the entire sermon is recorded in Matthew chapter 5:1 through chapter 7:28. In it Jesus explained what he expected of members of his kingdom. This address is the standard for Christian life. The parable is about anxiety and worry.

****

Anxiety is an extreme uneasiness of mind, even a brooding fear, about something that may or may not come to pass.

1. Have you ever been anxious? What does that feel like to you? According to Proverbs 12:25, how does anxiety affect a person?

2. Isaiah 35:4 tells us what we should do if we see others experiencing anxiety. What is that direction?

3. How can you claim Isaiah's advice in your own life? Consider memorizing Isaiah 35:4 and repeating it out loud when you are experiencing anxiety.

****

Before the Sermon on the Mount, Jesus was baptized by John. Following his baptism, Jesus fasted for 40 days alone in the wilderness. At the end of the 40 days, Satan approached Jesus and tempted him with riches beyond measure here on earth if Jesus would worship Satan. Jesus refused and Satan left him. After he heard that King Herod imprisoned John the Baptist, Jesus went to live in Capernaum on the northwest side of the Sea of Galilee. There, Jesus called several disciples and began his teaching and healing ministry.

Jesus was teaching in Galilee synagogues when news of him spread through the area. Large crowds followed him. Seeing the crowds, Jesus went to a mount and sat down. On the northwestern corner of the Sea of Galilee near Capernaum is a gently sloping hillside, often considered the Sermon location. The hillside would have been covered with grass interspersed with wildflowers. Possibly, Jesus sat at the bottom of the hillside while listeners sat in the grass at higher elevations similar to an amphitheater. Matthew wrote that Jesus's disciples came to him and he began to teach them. Most likely the "them" that Matthew identified referred to both Jesus's disciples and the crowd present.

In the Sermon on the Mount, Jesus included Beatitudes, what we are blessed by experiencing. He spoke about the salt of the earth and warned that if the salt lost its flavor it was good for nothing. Jesus gave God's standards for murder, adultery, divorce, and love of enemies. Matthew recorded that Jesus first spoke the Lord's Prayer in the Sermon on the Mount. In the parable of the lilies and the grass, Jesus seems to chide listeners. His exact words were:

> And why do you worry about clothes? See how the lilies of the field grow. They do not labor or spin. Yet I tell you that not even Solomon in all his splendor was dressed like one of these. If that is how God clothes the grass of the field, which is here today and tomorrow is thrown into the fire, will he not much more clothe you—you of little faith? (Matthew 6:28-30 NIV).

Jesus began this parable by asking listeners why they worried about clothes. In early Galilee, many individuals had no more than one-or-two sets of clothes. One set was for everyday wear and one for festive occasions. Jesus wasn't asking why individuals worried about *which* outfit they wore on a particular day. Instead he asked why they worried *if* they had clothes to wear.

Then, Jesus said that King Solomon in his splendor—in his rich, colorful garb—wasn't dressed as gloriously as a lily of the field, a simple field flower. In contrast to peasant's clothes made primarily from wool, goat hair, or camel chair, Solomon's clothes were made of linen, cotton, or silk. Often Solomon's outer mantle or robe was decorated with the fur of exotic animals. Solomon's clothes were usually purple, the symbol of royalty; however on special occasions, the king wore white garments to denote purity, cleanliness, and joy. Peasant clothes were undyed or dyed brown.

****

How many outfits do you have in your closet?

1. If you stop buying clothes for yourself for a year, would you be more or less anxious?

2. Estimate the amount of extra money you would save.

3. Imagine giving that money to a fund that provided food and clothing to orphans or widows, i.e. , Orphan Medical Network International (OMNI) or Samaritan's Purse. Seriously, how do you think you would feel about donating this amount to a Christian charity?

****

When Jesus used the lilies example, most likely he wasn't referring to the true lily described by the prophet Hosea. Instead, Jesus meant the anemone, a flower that grew wild and abundant in fields, was colorful, and known to most people. Often, anemones are called windflowers because even a gentle breeze will cause them to sway on their thin stalks. Anemones are perennials; they regrow year-after-year.

Anemone   Maria Lin

In Israel, the anemone blooms December through April. A single flower blooms on a leafless stalk. Normally, flowers have six petals. Most of these field flowers were red; however, anemone blossoms could be white, pink, purple, or blue. Flowers with red petals are most resistant to harsh growing conditions; they abound in Israel's steppes and deserts. Anemone flowers open in the morning and close in the evening. Although anemones have no nectar, flowers attract beetles and bees that feed on pollen.

The anemone has been associated with the Trinity, sorrow, and death; however, in the Sermon on the Mountain, the parable was about worry or anxiety. Three times in the Matthew 6:25-34 passage, Jesus told listeners not to worry. Specifically, Jesus identified four things they shouldn't worry about—their life, what they would eat, what they would drink, and what they would wear. Jesus promised that God knows his children's needs and God will meet those needs. Pragmatically, Jesus asked, "Who by worrying can add a single hour to his life" (Matthew 6:27 NIV)?

Stop reading right now! Go back and reread Jesus's question: can you add a single hour to your life, can you change a single outcome, can you increase or decrease what you have or don't have by worrying?

My aunt was a worrier, but she didn't just worry in her own mind, she worried out loud. We all heard her anxieties, her concerns, and even her dour predictions which worry generated. She lived a life of "what if." What if this happens, what if that happens. As a young girl, I didn't like to be around her. I didn't want to hear about all of the negative things that could happen. No, I'm not recommending that we keep our heads in the sand so to speak; however, remember the old saying that we don't need to borrow trouble by speculating about what could happen?

****

"Who by worrying can add a single hour to his life" (Matthew 6:27 NIV)?

1. By asking this question, what conclusion was Jesus trying to lead his listeners to?

2. How are you, more importantly, how could you apply the parable of the anemone to your life?

****

Have you ever seen wildflowers growing in a meadow as you drove along a little-used road? I have, and wondered why all this beauty was there? Why did God put beautiful flowers amidst this grass when so few people see them? Perhaps the answer is that God made the beauty for just one human—me(!) as I viewed it. On the other hand, perhaps God put the vibrant wildflowers in grassy meadows to remind himself that he knows every blade of grass, every flower, and every human.

Final Thoughts:
To my timeframe, wildflowers are transient. In God's timeframe I am transient. Why am I important to God?

Chapter 16
Growth of a Mustard Seed

Getting Started: Read Mark 4:30-32

Jesus seemed to like the mustard seed. He used it several times to illustrate parables and teachings. The current parable focus on the kingdom of God. This parable appeared in Matthew, Mark, and Luke. In Matthew it was placed between the parable of the weeds and Jesus's explanation of that parable.

Jesus was in Galilee when he told the parable of the mustard seed. Because Jesus grew up in a small village, he was aware of plants, their growth patterns, and their uses. He knew that mustard seeds are one of the smallest of all seeds; yet, this tiny seed grows into a tree big enough that birds perch on its branches. Here's how Mark recorded Jesus's parable:

> What shall we say the kingdom of God is like, or what parable shall we use to describe it? It is like a mustard seed, which is the smallest seed you plant in the ground. Yet when planted, it grows and becomes the largest of all garden plants, with such big branches that the birds of the air can perch in its shade (Mark 4:30-32 NIV).

Jesus used several parables to characterize the kingdom of God, i.e., the sower, wheat and tares, and leaven. This particular one illustrated the growth and expansion of God's kingdom on the earth. Although the church began in a small province of the Roman Empire, it grew rapidly to become larger than the mightiest empire on earth. The parable was prophetic, In it, Jesus described what was to come.

****

The growth of the Christian church was inevitable.

1. What direction did Jesus give to his disciples to grow the church? If you aren't sure, read the following verses, then, answer the question.

     a. Mark 16:15:
     b. Matthew 28:19:
     c. Acts 1:8:

2. What do you think Heaven will be like?

3. Is the Kingdom of God different from Heaven?

****

In African and Middle Eastern countries, the mustard tree is called the toothbrush tree. Indigenous to Persia (Iran), the mustard tree could entered Palestine along trade routes. Alternatively, returning Jewish exiles may have brought the tree seeds back from Persia and planted them in gardens and fields. The mustard tree is an evergreen shrub or tree that grows to 20 feet. Often mustard tree's many branches start low to the ground so that mustard trees grow as wide as tall. Mustard trees grow quickly and reach full size in a few years.

The mustard tree's growth pattern illustrated how the Christian church would grow. Like the branches of a mustard tree, Christianity spread wide, that is over the Roman Empire and even into India and Ethiopia. Similar to the fast growth of a mustard tree, Christianity flooded the ancient world. In a few centuries Christianity went from unheard of, to being outlawed, to the official religion of an empire.

Mustard tree pods

Mustard tree

Maria Lin

Many powerful men attempted to stop the spread of "The Way," the early name for the Christian church. The Jerusalem Jewish leadership tried to stop it when they arrested Jesus and turned him over to Pilate for crucifixion. Herod attempted to stifle the teaching of the apostles when he killed the apostle James and had Peter arrested. Paul was beaten, confined to house arrest, jailed, and finally murdered; however, his letters, many written when he was confined or jailed, formed the backbone of the spread of the good news of Jesus to the Gentile world. Jesus's parable of the mustard seed came true in the early centuries of the first millennia after Jesus's death.

****

Being a witness for Jesus

Use Mark 16:15, Matthew 28:19, and Acts 1:8 and answer the next three questions:

1.   It is the 21st century. Do Christians today need to spread the good news of Christ?

2.   What is the difference between being a witness of Christ with your words and with your behavior?

3.   There was an obituary about a woman that said she belong to x Christian church and was active in y and z Christian activities. A colleague told me that she worked with the woman every day for 23 years and didn't know she was a Christian. How would you feel if someone said that about you?

****

Mustard trees were used for shade because of their low-growing branches. Similarly, people from all nations took refuge under the canopy of Christianity. Unlike Jotham's thorn bush, the mustard tree had no thorns to deter people from resting beneath it. Although wild animals sometimes fed on tree shoots, many branches grew tall enough that predators couldn't reach birds that sat on them.

Think back on the Egyptian, Greek, and Roman empires. Each culture had so many gods and goddesses that it was almost impossible to remember who was who and who did what. Yet, I don't know any stories where a god died for the sins of a believer, or individuals who weren't yet believers. In contrast, the Christian religion has one God. God's son came to live on earth and then died for the sins of each man, woman, and child on earth at that time and for those who would be born in the future. Like a mustard tree providing shade to people and livestock, Christianity provides shade and protection for every individual on earth.

In Jesus's parable of the mustard tree, birds settled in its branches. Some Bible commentators took this clause as a warning to keep the early Christian church pure. In the ancient Near East, the phrase "birds of the air" was used to symbolize demonic forces in Scripture. When Jesus noted that birds settled in the mustard tree branches, he may have been warning disciples that Satan would attempt to encroach into the Kingdom of God.

Certainly, Jesus's warning became reality. Judaizers advocated that newly converted Christian could be justified only by observing Jewish laws, i.e., circumcision and adherence to dietary laws.

Further, Gnostics claimed to possess an elevated knowledge, a "higher truth." The higher knowledge was acquired not from the Bible or the apostles' teachings, but from a higher mystical plain of existence. Individuals with this special knowledge, for example, Jezebel in the Thyatiran church, believed they were elevated above other Christians because of their deeper knowledge of God (Revelation 2:18-25).

Importantly, the parable of the mustard seed remains true.. Even with the anti-Christian rhetoric of today and many churches turning from God's commands, continuation—even extension—of the church Jesus founded is inevitable.

My minister believes that the 21st century is more like the first century church than any other century in time. The Roman Empire and western civilizations are similar. Like the first century Roman Empire, westernized society embraces varied religious beliefs along with situational ethics and values. In the Roman Empire, Christian believers were under attack from non-believers and civil authorities alike. Today, claiming to be a Christian in western society causes ridicule, subtle, and, not so subtle, persecution. Often, first century Christians were and 21st century Christians are required by civilian law to participate in actions that conflict with their faith.

Throughout the Roman Empire, men, women, and children were persecuted and murdered because they acknowledge Christ as their Lord. Have you ever wondered why first century Christians, who suffered so severely for their faith, still remained believers and refused to deny they were Christians? I asked myself that question. Then, I recalled a recent television news clip in which 20 Christian men were beheaded with the beauty of the Mediterranean Sea as the backdrop. Their crime was belief in Jesus; they refuse to deny Jesus and convert to another religion. These men were no different than individual martyrs in first- and second-century Roman Empire.

The second-century Church father Tertullian wrote that "the blood of martyrs is the seed of the Church." Seeing a person stand firm in their faith despite slander, persecution, and even death often causes on-lookers to investigate that faith. Some come to a believing knowledge of Jesus. Thereby, more individuals rest under the canopy of the Christian church.

****

Will Christians be persecuted for their righteous actions?

1.   Read Matthew 5:10. What did Jesus say about being persecuted for righteous behavior? Was Jesus ever persecuted for his righteous behavior?

2.   Often, we don't recognize religious persecution. We believe that people are unkind because of some quirk in our personality. Don't be so quick to blame yourself when you are persecuted. Consider that you are being persecuted for your righteous behavior/standing for God.

3.   Identify 2-3 situations where you were persecuted for your personal righteous behavior.

****

At this time in the life of the Christian faith, it seems to be spreading more in developing countries (Africa, South America, Asia), than in westernized countries. Important for Christians is the answer to the question, "Where will Christianity inevitably spread and grow even deeper roots?" Will it be in Greece, Rome, or Spain, where Christianity was first embraced. Perhaps, Germany and Great Britain, homes to great reformation thought? What about the United States founded on principles of religious liberty? We need to pray that all countries experience revival in Christian thought so more individuals can rest in the shade of God's love.

Final Thoughts:
All Christians have a role to play in extending Jesus's message of salvation. Are you engaged in this role Jesus identified for you?

Chapter 17
Moving a Mulberry Tree

Getting Started: Read Luke 17:6

In a parable about a mulberry tree Jesus alluded to the power of faith. Although Matthew, Mark, and Luke, recorded several of Jesus's teachings on faith, this one-verse parable was recorded only by Luke. Probably, Peter told it to Luke.

****

"Now faith is being sure of what we hope for and certain of what we do not see" (Hebrews 11:1 NIV).

1.   Write down your definition of faith— that you have, not an idealized version.

2.   Look up the following verses about faith:

    a.   Romans 1:17
    b.   2 Corinthians 5:7
    c.   Hebrews 11:6
    d.   1Peter 1:7-9

3.   Rewrite your definition of faith. How did it change from question #1 to question #3?

****

When Jesus spoke the parable of the mulberry tree, he was talking privately to his disciples. Jesus outlined responsibilities for Christian discipleship. One responsibility was to never lead a person into sin. Jesus said it would be better for a disciple to be thrown into the sea with a millstone tied around his neck than to cause another to sin. A second responsibility was to rebuke a brother if he sins. The third responsibility—and perhaps the hardest—was to forgive a brother if he repents of sin and asks for forgiveness even as often as seven times a day. Seven times a day meant that the repentance-forgiveness cycle was limitless.

After hearing these requirements, disciples were overwhelmed with responsibilities as followers of Jesus. How could they live so blameless a life that they never caused another individual to sin? Did they have the courage to rebuke a fellow Christian when he or she sinned? How could they, simple men that they were, forgive and forgive and forgive? In desperation, the disciples cried out to Jesus, "Increase our faith!" (Luke17:5 NIV). The disciples wanted greater faith to live up to the standards Jesus set. Jesus gave them a one sentence response: "If you have faith as small as a mustard seed, you can say to this mulberry tree, 'Be uprooted and planted in the sea,' and it will obey you" (Luke 17:6 NIV)

The Greek word for faith used in this parable is *pistis*, which means moral conviction and reliance on Christ for salvation.[1] Also, p*istis* has a more abstract definition which includes "consistency." By using *pistis,* Jesus told disciples they could meet the responsibilities that he outlined through consistent reliance on him.

****

Most of us have faith in something.
1. Name some things or beings that you have faith in?

2. How do you exhibit this faith? In other words how do you act on your faith in these things or people?

3. How is having faith in the person of Jesus different from having faith in your church or your church doctrine?

****

Have you ever wondered why Jesus used a mulberry tree to illustrate the outcome of a small amount of consistent faith? If I wanted to illustrate the role of faith to move a tree, I would have used the largest tree I knew of, i.e., a cedar or the Tabor oak. Most likely,

Jesus chose a mulberry tree because one was nearby. Jesus said, "this mulberry tree," from which we can surmise that Jesus and his disciples were sitting under a mulberry tree or could see one from where they were seated.

The mulberry tree is also called the black mulberry and sycamine tree. In Israel, mulberry tree remains were found that dated from the late Iron Age.[7] Mulberry trees are popular in areas with long, hot summers to include areas of drought. The mulberry tree that can reach a height of 33 feet, but most times it is shorter. It has a short, stout trunk, and a broad canopy.

Mulberry trees grew throughout Judea and Galilee. Finding Jesus and disciples sitting under a mulberry tree is consistent with the tree's characteristics and growth pattern. During our stay at Kibbutz Lotan in the southern Negev Desert area, we saw a 25-foot-tall mulberry tree which was planted for shade.

Unlike many plant flowers, mulberry tree flowers are one sex or bisexual; sometimes flowers change from one sex to another. Mulberry trees were domesticated for their fruit; yet, trees don't bear much fruit before they are 15 years-of-age. Once fruiting starts, trees produces fruit for hundreds of years. Frequently, older mulberry trees produce better tasting fruit than younger trees. In the same way that a mulberry tree produces better tasting fruit with age, so Christians are often more spiritually productive after several (or many) years of studying God's word.

The genus name of the mulberry is derived from *mora* (Latin) meaning "delay,"[3] probably referring to the mulberry tree being the last tree to bud in the spring. Because the mulberry waits until all possibility of frost is past, it is called the "wisest of all trees."

Mulberry tree

Black Mulberry

Mama Lin

When his disciples asked Jesus to increase their faith, his response was that they could and would accomplish great tasks with a consistent small amount of faith in him. At that point in their walk with Jesus, probably the disciples didn't have unswerving faith in him. They were still getting to know Jesus and coming to realize that he was the promised Messiah. Jesus was wise enough to meet the disciples where they were in their awareness of him.

Because mulberry tree flowers bloom last in the spring doesn't mean that trees bloom late. Mulberry flowers bloom at just the right time to be fertile, pollinated, and produce mulberries each year. Have you ever noticed how God seems to time everything, i.e., events, relationships, etc. perfectly?

Back when Jesus told his disciples if they have as much faith as a mustard seed, they could move a mulberry tree, in essence Jesus was telling them: "You only need a little faith in me now." What he didn't tell them was that later, when he was arrested, crucified, and murdered, then was the time that they needed a lot of faith in him. A minister once told his congregation that "God is rarely early, but he is never late."

****

Does size matter? Is amount important?

My husband and I have a silly joke between the two of us. When I say to him that I am sorry for something, he asks me how much? Just sorry, very sorry, or very, very sorry? Are you just sorry or are you very, very sorry?

1. If you have to differentiate between a little faith and a lot of faith, how would you go about making that measurement?

2. Should you wait until your faith in Jesus is large, or fully mature, until you attempt to do something for Jesus, that is, you step out in faith?

3. How is it possible to have a lot of faith on one topic i.e., believe that Christ is the Savior of the world, while having only a little faith on another topic, i.e., if I tithe on my income before taxes, I will have enough money to pay my bills.

****

My husband and I had a long talk about consistent reliance on Jesus. Reliance means to be dependent because you have confidence based on experience. Reliance on Jesus doesn't come easy in today's society. We hear that religion is a crutch; as if we would fall down without religion. I'm not sure whether religion is or isn't a crutch for others, but I know that consistently relying on God isn't a crutch for me. It is the smartest thing I've ever done. Been there, done that, tried to live without Jesus at the center of my life. That time in my life was a total disaster. Talk about pain and mistakes!

Bruce said the same thing, i.e., before Jesus his life was out of control. After Jesus, reading the Bible, and implementing the Bible's guidelines for living, his life turned around. Our thoughts and lives didn't turn around all at once. Only as we spent consistently more time with God and developed the mind of Jesus did our behavior change. Now, we both intentionally and consistently put Jesus first in our lives, probably because we both have experienced what happened when we put ourselves first.

Final Thoughts:
Is faith logical? Is faith wishful thinking? Is faith the same as hope? What in the world is faith and why is it okay for me to have only a small amount of faith?

Chapter 18
Reeds Shaken by the Wind

Getting Started: Read Luke 7:18-28

John the Baptist's public ministry lasted only one to two years. Then, Herod Antipas arrested him. John was imprisoned at Machaerus, a fortress for political prisoners. While there, John sent several disciples to Jesus. They asked Jesus if he was the promised Messiah. After they left, Jesus contrasted John's firm convictions with reeds blown by the wind.

****

Contemplate the notion of firmness of convictions.

1. What is a conviction? Look up the word in a dictionary. List three of your convictions.

      a.

      b.

      c.

2. Is it possible to have a conviction that you don't hold to firmly? In the above list, highlight or check the ones that you don't firmly hold to.

3. Look at the remaining convictions. If you believe them and hold firmly to them, how do they impact your life?

****

Jesus went to John to be baptized. Although this baptism was the start of Jesus's public ministry, it was the high point of John's. Soon afterward, King Herod arrested John. The reason was that John criticized Herod for divorcing his powerful Nabatean queen to marry his sister-in-law, Herodias. Personally, Herod was indignant that John had the audacity to hold him—a king—to the same moral standards as everyone else.

The Bible recorded that King Herod used this personal reason for imprisoning John, however, getting John out of circulation made political sense. When John preached that individuals who came to him for baptism must change their behavior. John's demanded changes impacted King Herod's income. For example, John told tax collectors to collect only the amount of money required by Rome. They should stop lining their pockets and those of King Herod by over-taxing citizens. Likewise John taught that soldiers must be content with their pay and stop extorting money from people. John had tremendous influence with people in Herod's kingdom. According to Josephus, Herod feared that John, with his widespread support from the common people, would instigate rebellion against him.[8]

****

Compare and contrast John the Baptist and Jesus.

1. Consider how the two of them dressed, where they lived, who their friends were, the manner in which they spoke, etc.

2. Compare the behaviors of the civil and religious authorities toward each man.

3. Today, in America how do you think that we would treat John the Baptist? How would we treat Christ if he lived today?

****

After John was in prison perhaps 15-18 months, he sent two disciples to Jesus. They asked Jesus if he was the expected Messiah or if they should wait for someone else (Luke 7:19). Jesus didn't give the disciples a direct "Yes" or "No" answer. Instead Jesus told the disciples to go back to John and report what they saw and heard, i.e., the blind received their sight, the lame walked, and lepers were cured. After John's messengers left, Jesus asked the crowd what they expected when they went to see John in the desert. In his questioning Christ told a parable in which he contrasted John the Baptist's behavior with a reed that blew in the wind, swaying first one way than another. Here is how Luke recorded Jesus's parable:

> What did you go out into the desert to see? A reed swayed by the wind? If not, what did you go out to see? A man   dressed in fine clothes? No, those who wear expensive clothes and indulge in luxury are in palaces. But what did you go out to see? A prophet? Yes, I tell you, and more than a prophet. This is the one about whom it is written:" 'I will send my messenger ahead of you, who will prepare your way before you.' I tell you, among those born of women there is no one greater than John; yet the one who is least in the kingdom of God is greater than he. (Luke 7:24-28 NIV).

The reed that Jesus referred to when talking about John was the Israeli reed, sometimes called the giant reed and Cypress cane. Reed colonies were located on the banks of natural water courses, in floodplains of medium or large sized streams, and in dry riverbanks far from permanent water sources. Reeds grew throughout Israel from Mount Hermon to the Negev Desert.

The giant reed is a perennial; it comes up year-after-year. Reeds can grow to 20 feet and may grow 10-12 feet in a single growing season. The central reed stalk is called a culm; culms are about one and a half inches in diameter and hollow. Each culm has leaves that resemble those on corn stalks; however, leaves have sharp edges that can cut fingers. As drier weather prevailed, foliage turned light brown and rattled in the wind. Giant reeds bend with the wind, even when they grow in large colonies. In ancient times, and even today, reeds were used as wind breaks and to stop soil erosion.

Israeli Reed   Maria Lin

Individuals who came to John for baptism knew about reeds; they saw reeds growing along the Jordan River. To them reeds elicited mainly positive thoughts. Probably, they remembered how Isaiah associated reeds with humility (Isaiah 58:5). But, Jesus denied that John was similar to a swaying reed; instead, John was firm and upright. Jesus averred that John's beliefs were certain and John lived by them. John stayed on message (repentance) and on task, i.e., baptism. John didn't have a politically correct bone in his body. He didn't pander to public opinion, giving one message to common people and a second one to the rich and powerful. John called the Jerusalem elite "a brood of vipers."

Although Jesus denied that John was a swaying reed, John's purpose reflected how reeds were used in ancient Judea and Galilee. By his words and life, John stood against the erosion of godly behavior. He called ordinary citizens, tax collectors, and civil and religious leaders to change their lives to reflect God's standards. Also, like reeds used as windbreaks, John stood as a buffer between people who were righteous and the secular society of the Roman Empire. The best windbreaks lower wind chill in man, animals, and plants. Everything we know about John the Baptist showed a priest and prophet who lived close to God. As a windbreak, John lowered the chilling effects of a secular Roman society on inhabitants of Galilee and Judea.

The spiritual interpretation of Jesus's parable included a eulogy for John. In addition to commendatory words given at a memorial service, eulogy means "high praise." King Herod had not yet murdered John; however, Jesus eulogized John by saying of all the men (and by extension women) born of woman, there was none greater than John the Baptist. John was no weak reed, or as we would say in modern times, "no shrinking violet."

****

What do you want in your eulogy?

1. List several characteristics you want to be remembered for, i.e., you were a woman of character, you were a man who loved his family, you were loyal, etc.

2. Now that you have identified what you want to be remembered for, what do you think will be said in your eulogy?

3. Starting today, what can you change about yourself to make your eulogy be what you would like it to be?

****

Final Thoughts:
Given Jesus's high words of praise for
John the Baptist, propose reasons that
churches don't give John more
attentions.

Chapter 19
Lost Son and Carob Pods

Getting Started: Read Luke 15:11-32

The parable of the lost son is one of Jesus's longer parables. It was the last of three parables in which Jesus made the point that God searches for the lost, whether a sheep, coin, or person. In the parable, plant pods were mentioned, seemingly in passing; however, the pods played a role in incentivizing the lost son to return home to his father. For years, the parable of the lost son was called the parable of the prodigal son. Prodigal means a person who spends lavishly or foolishly or returns after an absence. Both titles reflect the younger son's behavior.

****

Which one of the sons do you identify with in this parable – the older or younger son? Explain your reasoning.

****

The context for the parable of the lost son is vital to understanding and interpreting it. At the time a large crowd was following Jesus as he traveled from Galilee southward to Jerusalem. Some in the crowd believed what Jesus taught; others wanted to see him perform a great miracle. Pharisees traveled in the group. Carefully, they watched Jesus's behavior and listened to what he said to learn if he did or said anything that contradicted Jewish law. Pharisee means loyal to God and separated one; however their behavior didn't reflect the meaning their name. They were extremists in adhering to a limited portion of the Hebrew law, while ignoring the remainder of it. Pharisees were the most influential Jewish group in Palestine and the most bitter and deadly opponents of Jesus and his message.

At this particular time, Luke recorded that tax collectors and other sinners gathered around Jesus. The Pharisees and teachers of the law started to mutter that Jesus welcomed sinners and even ate with them. In response Jesus told three parables. The first two were relatively short and focused on a man who lost a sheep and a woman who lost a silver coin. Both items were valuable and owners searched diligently for them. When found, their owners rejoiced. Probably, the tax collectors, sinners, and Pharisees all nodded when they heard Jesus tell these two parables. Correctly, they interpreted the parables to mean that God searches for the lost; however, Jesus's third parable—the parable of the lost son—had a different ending. Here is what Jesus said:

> There was a man who had two sons. The younger one said to his father, "Father, give me my share of the estate." So he divided his property between them. Not long after that, the younger son got together all he had, set off for a distant country and there squandered his wealth in wild living. After he had spent everything, there was a severe famine in that whole country, and he began to be in need. So he went and hired himself out to a citizen of that country, who sent him to his fields to feed pigs. He longed to fill his stomach with the pods that the pigs were eating, but no one gave him anything.

> When he came to his senses, he said, "How many of my father's hired men have food to spare, and here I am starving to death! I will set out and go back to my father and say to him: 'Father, I have sinned against heaven and against you. I am no longer worthy to be called your son; make me like one of your hired men'" (Luke 15:11-19 NIV).

****

Substitute means to exchange, switch, or replace with something else.

1.   Substitute is what the younger son did in this parable. He substituted his life as a valued son for a life of shameful living and feeding pigs. He replaced eating the best foods with longing to have carob pods to eat.

2. Often we hear or read that Jesus was the substitute for the sins of many (men and women). What does that even mean? How does that work for me and you as individuals? Was Jesus really the substitute for my individual sin? Did he receive what I should deserve to receive?

3. What if I tell Jesus not to bother with me. I am okay on my own, like the Pharisees thought their righteousness met God's requirements for salvation? Am I really okay on my own?

****

After the lost son came to his senses and decided to act, most of us can imagine him immediately acting. I don't think that this son gave his employer a two-weeks-notice:

> So he got up and went to his father. But while he was still a long way off, his father saw him and was filled with compassion for him; he ran to his son, threw his arms around him and kissed him. The son said to him, "Father, I have sinned against heaven and against you. I am no longer worthy to be called your son."

> But the father said to his servants, "Quick! Bring the best robe and put it on him. Put a ring on his finger and sandals on his feet. Bring the fattened calf and kill it. Let's have a feast and celebrate. For this son of mine was dead and is alive again; he was lost and is found." So they began to celebrate (Luke 15:17-24 NIV).

So far, so good! The parable sounded the same as that of the lost sheep and lost coin. Listening tax collectors and sinners, who identified with the younger son, rejoiced to hear that God forgave them unconditionally. Even the Pharisees and teachers of the law had no criticism of Jesus's words at this point. They believed that repentant sinners could be restored to full fellowship with God.

If Jesus had stopped there, all would have been well. What Jesus said next offended and further alienated the Pharisees. Here are Jesus exact words as recorded by Luke:

> Meanwhile, the older son was in the field. When he came near the house, he heard music and dancing. So he called one of the servants and asked him what was going on.
>
> "Your brother has come," he replied, "and your father has killed the fattened calf because he has him back safe and sound."
>
> The older brother became angry and refused to go in. So his father went out and pleaded with him. But he answered his father, "Look! All these years I've been slaving for you and never disobeyed your orders. Yet you never gave me even a young goat so I could celebrate with my friends. But when this son of yours who has squandered your property with prostitutes comes home, you kill the fattened calf for him!"
>
> 'My son," the father said, "you are always with me, and everything I have is yours. But we had to celebrate and be glad, because this brother of yours was dead and is alive again; he was lost and is found' (Luke 15:25-32 NIV).

When Jesus finished the parable, listeners knew that the older brother was the Pharisees. Jesus's parable exposed the Pharisees for what they were, i.e., hard hearted, self-righteous prigs, who believed that their lifestyle earned them special merit before Father God. In their opinion everything they did was right. God was happy to have them as believers and would welcome them into his kingdom. Similar to the older son looking down on the younger, Pharisees looked down on tax collectors, prostitutes, and sinners. Pharisees had no awareness of their need for a Savior. Their high opinion of themselves wouldn't let them believe that Jesus considered them spiritually impoverished.

****

At about age 11 I accepted Christ as my Savior and most of the time attempted to live for God after that. When I read the story of the prodigal (lost) son, I always identified with the older son, thinking that God would regard me higher than a person who repented later in life. I was as self-righteous as the older son and the listening Pharisees.

1. Can you think of a time when you thought you were righteous or acted self-righteously. Describe your thoughts and actions.

****

The pods that the unrepentant son longed to eat were carob pods, the fruit of the carob tree. Likely, carob trees were brought from Babylon by Jewish exiles when they returned to Judea. In ancient Israel, carob trees were also called John's bread and locust. When John the Baptists lived in the wilderness, he ate locust and wild honey. Possibly, he ate carob pods rather than locust insects. Carob trees grew wild throughout Palestine to include in desert areas.

Carob trees are small; typically, they grew to 33 feet. Leaves are evergreen. Carob pods contain a soft pale-brown pulp and 10-13 flat, hard seeds. When the fruit is fully ripe and dry, pods are light-to-dark brown and seeds rattle in the pod. Before winter rains, pods are picked from trees or shaken loose from limbs using a long pole with a terminal hook. In Bible times pods were used to feed livestock. Carob trees produced pods even in times of drought and famine.

In Jesus's parable, the Gentile farmer didn't give food to the pig keeper. The young man was so hungry that he longed to fill his stomach with the carob pods fed to the pigs. Probably, he didn't eat carob pods because he belief that carobs were fodder for animals, not food for man. In reality, the young man could have eaten both the carob pods and seeds.

Carob branch   Maria Lin

Today, carob pods are dried, roasted, and ground into carob flour. Often the flour or powder is a substitute for chocolate. Carob pods are naturally sweet, low in fat, high in fiber, has calcium, and unlike chocolate has no caffeine. Carob pods are used as a thickener in bakery goods, ice cream, and salad dressings. In May at a kibbutz in the southern Negev Desert, I ate a ripe carob pod left on a tree from earlier in the growing season. It was fibrous and tasted sweet, a little like cocoa.

****

What does it take in our lives to admit we God's need his help?
1.   In the story of the lost son, do you think the son would have returned to his father if he had sufficient food to eat at his job feeding pigs?

2. Is it fair for a person who lied and cheated all his life to turn to God in the final days or hours of his life and be saved?

3. Consider the thief on the cross: Aren't you annoyed, just a little bit annoyed, that the thief is going to go to heaven after how he acted most of his life?

****

I wonder if Pharisees ever had an experience similar to the younger son. Likely, they never went hungry. They never found themselves so destitute that they hired themselves out to feed a Gentile's pigs. Mosaic Law declared that swine were unclean (Deuteronomy 14:8). Tending pigs was a degrading activity for an Israelite man. Yet, hunger, despair, absence of self-esteem, and not knowing that God welcomes repentant sons and daughters with open arms, caused the younger son and causes many individuals today to feed pigs rather than eat at God's banquet table.

Final Thoughts
When the younger son asked the father for his inheritance, he told his father, "I wish you were dead." When we reject God to pursue our own desires, we tell God, "You are dead to me."

Chapter 20
Virgins with Oil Lamps

Getting Started: Read Matthew 25:1-13

The parable of ten virgins emphasizes the importance of being prepared for Jesus to return to earth the second time. Preparation includes planning. For the 10 young virgins, preparation included having sufficient olive oil to fuel their lamps. Last spring, I sold my Christian books at a "Prepper's Convention." Vendors were selling everything imaginable to prepare buyers for natural or manmade disasters, i.e., dried food, batteries, small stoves, guns, and ammunition. Seeing the hundreds of participants caused me to think about Jesus's second coming and preparation for it. If all these individuals could prepare for disaster, surely I could prepare for the greatest future event ever to come, the second coming of Jesus.

****

Christians must prepare their minds for action!

When Peter exhorted individuals in the scattered Christian church to prepare their minds for action (1 Peter 1:13-16), he wasn't recommending a contemplative lifestyle, only attending a Bible study, or listening to Christian radio. Peter expected action from Christians as they waited for Jesus to come.

1. Read 1 Peter 1:13-16, what did Peter expect Christians to do?

    a.
    b.

c.

d.

2. Are you doing what Peter exhorted you to do?

****

Beginning with Adam and Eve, God-fearing individuals looked for a coming Messiah. Abraham and about 500 years later Moses believed that God would send the Messiah. As years turned into decades, decades to centuries, and centuries to millennium, many Jews believed that the notion of a coming Messiah was a myth. The last prophet in the Old Testament, Malachi (440-430 BC) recorded a hypothetical conversation between God and men of Israel (Malachi 3:13-18). One group identified that it was futile to serve God and carry out his requirements. Arrogant, evildoers prospered. The redemption (Messiah) that good men looked for had not appeared even after many centuries.

Another group of men feared and followed God. God wrote their names in a scroll of remembrance, similar to a record of notable deeds kept by earthly kings (Esther 6:1-6; Isaiah 4:3). God promised that on judgement day these men would be spared and separated from those men who didn't serve him.

Jesus told the parable of the 10 virgins to his disciples to reinforce Malachi's teaching. At the time Jesus was seated on the Mount of Olives. It was Passover week. In a few days, Jerusalem's Jewish leaders would capture Jesus, turn him over to Pilate, and demand that the Romans crucify him. Here is the parable:

> The kingdom of heaven will be like ten virgins who took their lamps and went out to meet the bridegroom. Five of them were foolish and five were wise. The foolish ones took their lamps but did not take any oil with them. The wise, however, took oil in jars along with their lamps.

The bridegroom was a long time in coming, and they all became drowsy and fell asleep. At midnight the cry rang out: "Here's the bridegroom! Come out to meet him!" Then all the virgins woke up and trimmed their lamps. The foolish ones said to the wise, "Give us some of your oil; our lamps are going out."

"No," they replied, "there may not be enough for both us and you. Instead, go to those who sell oil and buy some for yourselves."

But while they were on their way to buy the oil, the bridegroom arrived. The virgins who were ready went in with him to the wedding banquet. And the door was shut. Later the others also came. "Sir! Sir!" they said. "Open the door for us!"

But he replied, "I tell you the truth, I don't know you." Therefore keep watch, because you do not know the day or the hour (Matthew 25:1-13 NIV).

The plant identified in the parable of the virgins was the olive tree. Olive oil fueled the lamps of the waiting virgins. The olive tree is one of the world's oldest cultivated trees. The olive tree is indigenous to present day Israel and Syria. Its dry composition makes the olive tree drought tolerant. Olive trees live up to 1000 years. Very old trees can be hollow, secondary to fungus having attack the wood. Leaves appear gray-green on top, while the bottom has a silvery appearance.

The olive is oval shaped and contains a seed. Usually, unripe olives are green and ripe olives are purple-black. Olives ripen in the Hebrew month of Ab (Av, the 11th month of the Hebrew calendar) which corresponds to July–August on the western calendar. Ancient peoples used long sticks to shake olive tree branches with the result that ripe olives fell to the ground. Ripe olives were gathered and those allocated for oil were put into an olive press. Ancient olive presses were heavy hewed stones with a vertical stone wheel. The wheel was rotated by an animal (donkey or ox) or by persons. The oil and watery liquid squeezed from the pulp was separated in settling vats. Water sank to the bottom while oil floated on the top. Oil was drained through a linen cloth to remove impurities. Lamps such as the bridesmaids used required large amounts of oil to keep them burning. Often oil had to be replenished as often as every 15 minutes (Matthew 25:9 NIV notes).

Olive oil had a central place in Israelite history. In the Tabernacle, olive oil was the fuel for the seven Lamps on the Golden Candlestick. Olive oil was used to anoint and set apart kings, priest, and prophets. In ancient Palestine, olive oil was used for healing, i.e., the Good Samaritan used olive oil to heal the wounds of the man who was robbed and beaten on his way to Jericho. In the early Christian church, olive oil symbolized the illuminating presence of the Holy Spirit. Through the Holy Spirit's presence, Christian actions shines in a dark world, healing the world.

****

The Holy Spirit illuminates a Christian's life.

The Hebrew word for olive tree, olive, and olive oil was *zayith* which means yielding illuminating oil.[1] Read, ponder, and discuss how the Holy Spirit illuminates or should illuminate your life. Some Bible verses that will aid you are:

    a. John 14:16-18
    b. John 16:8-13
    c. Hebrews 10:16

****

Olive tree

oil lamp

Maria Lin

The parable of the virgins with their lamps used imagery from wedding customs of first century Palestine. The wedding feast took place in the evening; the day was filled with dancing and entertainment. At the day's end, the bridegroom along with his good friends went to the home of the bride's parents. The bride left her parent's home and joined her bridegroom. They headed to the groom's home to a banquet held in their honor. Friends joined the groom and bride along the way to their home. Often, the procession was halted along the way for the couple to receive congratulations or share a toast. Eventually, the bride and groom reached the groom's home and enter it. The door was closed and the wedding feast began.

Some Bibles translate the 10 virgins as bridesmaids who were typically girls younger than the bride. Perhaps, they were 10-11 years old. If these girls were bridesmaids, for some reason they weren't a part of the groom and bride's procession. Rather, they waited at the groom's home. The bridal party was delayed; it didn't arrive until around midnight. The young bridesmaids fell asleep. The noise from the approaching bridal party woke them. Each trimmed her lamp—cut down the wick so the lamp wouldn't smoke. Five wise bridesmaids anticipated a delay in the bridal party's arrival. They brought an extra flask of oil to keep their lamps burning. The other five bridesmaids failed to bring extra oil.

In this parable the bridesmaids were central figures; however, their number isn't important. Because the parable of the virgins identified an equal number of wise and foolish virgins doesn't mean that there will be an equal number of righteous and unrighteous individuals on earth at Jesus's second coming. Likely, Jesus gave the figure to round out the story.

In the Bible, the bridegroom is synonymous with Jesus, the Christ. Often the bride is the Christian church, composed of all who believe Jesus is the son of God and acknowledge him as Lord of their life (1 John 5:12). The interpretation of the parable of the virgins is that when Jesus comes the second time, it will be too late to rethink our lives or initiate a "do over" of life. At this time, Jesus's followers will enter into the wedding banquet with the bridegroom. They will have eternal live with God. The unprepared and foolish, who rejected or ignored Jesus, will be shut out; they will endure eternal punishment (Matthew 25:46).

The parable of the 10 virgins wasn't about the son of God's first coming to earth. It is about his return to earth a second time. In the parable of the ten virgins, Jesus continued his assertion from Matthew chapter 24 that only God knows when Jesus's second coming will occur. The parable is one of three, i.e., parable of the ten virgins, talents, and the sheep and goats, with the same message. All emphasized the truth that Jesus will come a second time and the importance of being spiritually prepared.

****

Both the Boy and Girl Scout mottos are "Be prepared."

1. That Scout motto means that scouts must be ready, willing, and able to do what is necessary in any situation that comes along, even in an emergency. Prepared means to plan in advance, make ready beforehand, and to work out the details. How could you use the Scout motto in your life as you wait for Jesus's second coming?

2. What do you have to plan so you will be ready for Jesus's second arrival? Alternatively, are you right where you should be and need no different preparation?

3. Probably, scouts prepare for an emergency by taking a cardiopulmonary resuscitation (CPR) class. List changes or actions you need to take to be optimally prepared for Jesus's second coming.

    a.

    b.

    c.

****

In first century Palestine, only a minority of Jews still looked for the promised Messiah. Even fewer understood that Jesus, the Messiah, would come a second time. Generally, Jesus's disciples believed that his second coming would be soon after his ascension, even within their lifetimes. But, decades passed, decades turned into centuries, and centuries into millennia. For us living in the 21st century, it is easy to doubt that Jesus will come again. It's easy to fall asleep waiting for Jesus's second coming. It is easy to be unprepared, to stop planning ahead, so that if Jesus's return is delayed (by our standards of promptness), we are caught unaware and unprepared. When Jesus returns, individual preparedness will count. Preparedness can't be shared or transferred just as the wise virgins couldn't share their oil with the foolish ones.

Final Thoughts:
Malachi's point was that fearing and serving God and looking for the Messiah wasn't futile. These activities had long-term rewards. Similarly, for Christians living a life consistent with God's laws and statutes now will have long-term rewards.

Chapter 21
In-grafted Wild Olive Branch

Getting Started: Read Romans 11:16-24

Despite Jewish Christians starting the Christian Church in Rome, Gentile Christians resisted accepting Jewish Christians into their fellowship. Paul's letter to the Romans (about 71 AD) included a parable using cultivated olive and wild olive trees to illustrate Gentile's proper response to their Jewish Christian brethren.

Initially, the church in Rome was composed of Jews who believed that Jesus was the Messiah. The Church in Rome wasn't started by an apostle, but by Jews who returned from Pentecost in Jerusalem (Acts 2). Almost immediately, Jewish believers evangelized Gentiles. Then, Emperor Claudius banished all Jews from Rome. For 12 years the Christian church in Rome consisted of only Gentiles.

When Nero became Emperor, he invited Jews back to Rome, noting that they were good for business and trade. The problem was that Gentiles refused to allow Jewish Christians back into the Christian church in Rome. Perhaps, Gentile Christians concluded that Emperor Claudius's rejection of the Jewish Christians meant that God also rejected them. Because Rome was the capital city of the Roman Empire, this discriminatory attitude had the potential to spread beyond Rome.

****

Imagine yourself as Jewish Christian who started the church in Rome.

1. How would you feel about this church—this body of believers in Rome? Would you be emotionally tied to them? Feel you have a vested interest in the church?

2. Ponder your feelings when you returned to your home church in Rome after 12 years of forced exile only to find that you weren't welcome when you returned. Identify, record, and verbalize how you as a Jewish Christian would have felt. Summarize your feelings.

3. How would Paul's parable in Romans 11 make you feel more or less secure?

****

Paul focused his evangelistic efforts on the Gentiles, that is, all individuals who weren't Jews. He named himself the apostle to the Gentiles. Paul spent years journeying throughout the Roman Empire converting Gentiles and strengthening their commitment to Jesus as Christ (the Messiah, the son of God).

In Paul's letter to the church in Rome, Paul made it clear that the current parable was designed for Gentile believers (Romans 11:13). He wrote it to counter Roman Gentile's arrogant belief that they were better than Jewish Christians. One basis for Gentile arrogance was that unlike Jews, Gentiles didn't reject Jesus and lobby for his crucifixion. Further, the Gentile converts never denied that Jesus rose from the dead as many Jerusalem Jewish leaders denied the resurrection. Here is the parable of grafting wild olive branches onto a cultivated olive root that Paul wrote to the Romans:

> If the root is holy, so are the branches. If some of the branches have been broken off, and you, though a wild olive shoot, have been grafted in among the others and now share in the nourishing sap from the olive root, do not boast over those branches. If you do, consider this: You do not support the root, but the root supports you. You will say then, "Branches were broken off so that I could be grafted in." Granted. But they were broken off because of unbelief, and you stand by faith. Do not be arrogant, but be afraid. For

if God did not spare the natural branches, he will not spare you either.

Consider therefore the kindness and sternness of God: sternness to those who fell, but kindness to you, provided that you continue in his kindness. Otherwise, you also will be cut off. And if they do not persist in unbelief, they will be grafted in, for God is able to graft them in again. After all, if you were cut out of an olive tree that is wild by nature, and contrary to nature were grafted into a cultivated olive tree, how much more readily will these, the natural branches, be grafted into their own olive tree! (Romans 11:16-24 NIV).

In the parable of the in-grafted wild olive branch, Paul identified a) a root and branches (boughs) of a cultivated olive tree, b) a branch (bough) of a wild olive tree, and c) grafting a wild olive branch onto a cultivated olive tree. The original cultivated olive tree with its root and branches is the promises God made to Abraham, Isaac, Jacob, and their offspring, the Jews. This root was solid and sure.

Jews who believed in Jesus as Messiah were the original root and branches of the early Christian church. Branches broken off from the cultivated olive tree were Jews who refused to believe that Jesus was the long looked for Messiah. This was the majority of Jews who lived in Palestine and throughout the Roman Empire at the time. The wild olive branch equated to Gentile Christians who believed that Jesus was the son of God and followed his teachings. The interpretation of Paul's parable in Romans chapter 11 is that the Gentile believers were grafted into—became an integral, productive off shoot—of the Jewish faith.

****

Imagine yourself as a Gentile Christian, a member of the church in Rome.

1. Would you have been secretly glad to see the Jewish Christians leave town? After all, now the group would be more homogenous, all would be Gentiles.

2. When the Jewish Christians returned to Rome and wanted to again fellowship in the Christian church, what would have been your response–anger, disdain, resentment, even fear that the returning Jews would try to take over the church?

3. How would Paul's parable in Romans 11 make you feel more or less secure?

****

Although Paul's parable seems easy to interpret, it has nuances that are only made clear by understanding characteristics of both cultivated and wild olive trees and the grafting process in olive trees. Paul identified that a wild olive branch was grafted onto the root of the cultivated olive tree; however, olive growers rarely graft wild olive branches onto cultivated olive trees. In nature, just the opposite occurs: growers graft cultivated olive tree branches onto wild olive tree roots. Paul was aware of this normal grafting procedure. Paul wrote that his parable was contrary to nature (Romans 11:24). Perhaps, Paul believed that making his point was more important than technical accuracy about olive tree grafting.

Horticulturists identify three reasons for tree grafting: 1) to propagate trees that don't root well by cutting a shoot from the poorly growing tree and grafting it onto a healthy tree; 2) to obtain a stronger root system, and 3) to grow plants faster. Importantly, the root sustains the newly grafted branch; the newly grafted branch doesn't sustain the root.

In Paul's parable, all three reasons support grafting the newly converted Gentile believers into roots of Judaism. Gentiles used the structures and traditions of the established Jewish faith as roots for their worship of Jesus. An example is the Jewish tradition of meeting weekly to hear and study God's word. Using this Jewish tradition, new Christian church members fellowshipped regularly and became more knowledgeable about their faith. Further, Jews had sacred God-inspired writings. Knowing about and hearing Jewish scriptures (Old Testament) facilitated more ready acceptance of the New Testament gospel and letters. In these ways, the Christian faith grew stronger and faster and became a deeper part of Gentile-convert's lives. The new Gentile believers and churches acquired spiritual richness and fertility by being grafted into the deeply rooted, cultivated olive tree (Jewish faith).

Although the cultivated olive tree formed the root and some branches of the olive tree in Paul's parable, the in-grafted wild olive tree branch resonates with most of us. We are the wild olive branch. Today, Gentile believers form most of the body of believers in churches in westernized countries.

Common names for the wild olive tree are oleaster and Russian olive. Wild olive trees are often 12-15 feet tall, so they are more often a shrub than tree. Wild olive trees are multi-trunked and often grow as wide as tall. Wild olive trees grow almost everywhere, e.g., brackish water and river bottoms where water level is seldom more than two feet below ground surface. They are drought tolerant and indifferent to wind and heat. The spreading growth pattern and diversity of growth sites of wild olive trees mirrored the growth of the new Christian church. Gentiles (non-Jewish) were almost everywhere in the Roman Empire. The Christian church appeared and thrived even in the most unhospitable environments.

The wild olive tree has deep taproot (central root) and well-developed lateral roots. As it looks for water, the wild olive sinks it main root deep into the soil, while spreading horizontal in search of nutrients. This diverse root system adds to the stability of the wild olive tree. About 80% of the United States population self-identifies as Christians. Like the wild olive tree, many have a root deep in their Christian faith. At the same time, they aren't necessarily tied to one church denomination. They spread horizontal roots in search of an optimal church family.

Wild olive tree branch   Maria Lin

Like the cultivated olive tree, the wild olive produces a drupe-like fruit; however, fruit is smaller than and not as tasty as olives from cultivated olive trees. In most countries, wild olives aren't eaten. Generally, the fruit isn't used to make olive oil. In Paul's parable, a wild olive branch was grafted onto a cultivated olive tree; however, the wild olive branch would never produces the same olive that grows on a cultivated olive tree. Similarly, Christianity is a unique religion and doesn't produce the same fruit as Judaism.

****

In your church do you have tiers of individuals, i.e., some who are more important than others?

Using Paul's carefully written words in the entire Romans 11 chapter and particularly the parable of the in-grafted wild olive branch, answer the following questions.

1. What groups are more important than other groups in your church?

2. What groups are you in? Describe, discuss, and explain your conclusions. As you write or verbalize your answer, forget about a "socially acceptable" response, or even a "Christian" response. Write/verbalize your true feelings.

3. What do you think Paul would conclude about your church from your answers?

****

Despite the seeming lesser value of wild olive tree products than cultivated olive tree products, Paul's parable didn't mean that Jewish Christians were more valuable than Gentile Christians. Similarly, although Jewish Christians were represented by branches (more than one) and Gentile Christians by a single branch didn't mean that there were more Jews than Gentiles in the Christian church at Rome. Probably, the opposite was true. Data aren't available for the number of Jews who became believers in the early centuries after Christ's death; but, by the early 21st century, the vast majority of Christians were Gentiles. Globally, less than one-half percent of Jews self-identify as Messianic Jews, that is, Jews who believe in Jesus as Messiah.

Paul's purpose in writing the parable of the in-grafted wild olive branch was to remind Gentile believers that the root of the Christian faith was in God's covenants with the Jews, God promised to bless all nations through Abraham's seed. When he reminded the Rome church about God's promise, Paul's wanted to encourage a fully integrated church. Paul wasn't attempting to make the Christian church in Rome a sect of Judaism, nor was he advocating that Gentile Christians replaced the Jews in God's favor.

Final Thoughts:
Is Christianity an inclusive or an exclusive faith?

Chapter 22
Productive versus Thorn-Infested Land

Getting Started: Read Hebrews 6:7-8

The Hebrews' author inserted a short two-verse parable to aid reader's intuitive understanding of a more difficult Christian truth (Hebrews 6:4-6). He believed that an agricultural parable about land producing crops versus thorns and thistles was an illustration that even the most urban reader in the first century could understand.

Hebrews was addressed to Jewish Christians, but, was relevant to Gentile Christians as well. For centuries biblical scholars believed that Paul wrote the letter to the Hebrews. Within the past 500 years other writers, i.e., Barnabas and Apollos, have been proposed. Who wrote Hebrews isn't as important as its message.

Immediately prior to the parable of productive versus non-productive land, the writer reprimands readers because they were slow to learn (Hebrews 5:11-14). He wants them to become more mature in their faith, moving beyond learning or relearning elementary teachings about Jesus and Christianity to more mature doctrine (Hebrews 6:1-2).

****

What do you expect a bean plant to produce?
What do you expect a fig tree to produce?
What do you expect a thorn tree to produce?

Read Matthew 7:15-20, then answer the following questions:

1. How can you differentiate between a good tree and a bad tree? What about a good and bad person?

2. Can thornbushes produce grapes and fruit? How do bad people produce good fruit?

3. What will God do to a tree that doesn't produce good fruit? What should a Christian do to a purported Christian that doesn't produce good fruit?

****

In Hebrews 6:4-6 are statements that include some of the most hotly contested beliefs among Christian scholars, not to mention among Christian church denominations. The writer asked: can an individual who has rejected Christ, after he has been enlightened and shared in the blessings of the Holy Spirit, be brought back to repentance? He averred that these believers—who have fallen away—crucify Jesus all over again and subject Jesus to public disgrace. Then, the writer provided a parable to illustrate his point:

> Land that drinks in the rain often falling on it and that produces a crop useful to those for whom it is farmed receives the blessing of God. But land that produces thorns and thistles is worthless and is in danger of being cursed. In the end it will be burned. (Hebrews 6:7-8 NIV).

Notice that the subject of the parable is the land – not rain, nor a farming process, not a crop, not a farmer, but land. The land receives rain and does something with the rain. In one instance the land responds by producing a useful crop. In other words, the land produced grains, trees, herbs, etc. that gave the farmer food for his family. Possibly, the crop was abundant enough so that some food could be sold, thereby enhancing food security for an entire community. In contrast, other land responds to the rain by producing thorns and thistles. This land is worthless to the farmer. It is in danger of being cursed. In the end it will be burned.

When my parents planted our garden in the 1960s, they first turned over the soil with a gas-operated, two-handled rototiller. Then, neat, straight rows (Dad was vehement that they be straight) were plowed for seeds. After children hand dropping seeds, Dad and Mom covered the seeds using a hoe.

Jesus's parable of the sower and seed could have been the impulse for the Hebrews' parable (Matthew 13:3-23). In that parable, the farmer broadcast his seed. My Dad and Mom would have been horrified at the waste of good seed! Notice what happened to the broadcast seed but pay particular attention to the seed that fell among thorns.

Some seed fell on the pathways. On pathways the soil was packed down by people who walked those paths. Some pathway seed was eaten by birds. The analogy is to a person who hears the good news about Christ, but shrugs it off. What Jesus did for him or her doesn't penetrate into their head or heart. Governor Felix in Acts chapter 24 is an example of seeds that fell along the pathway. Despite hearing Paul preach several times, Felix wouldn't commit to Christ as Savior.

Some seed fell on thin soil. When soil is thin, it can't support the plant's root structure or retain water. Soon after the plant rises through topsoil, the sun's scorching heat kills it. Some individuals who hear the gospel get all excited and decide they belief it. They may even make a profession of faith in Christ; but, because their commitment is superficial, almost immediately they return to their old beliefs, old ways of thinking, and old ways of behaving. The sorcerer Simon reflects seed that fell on thin soil (Acts 8:9-25). Likely, Simon was even baptized; however, his attempt to purchase the power to lay hands on converts so he could impute the Holy Spirit to them demonstrated an almost immediate return to his old ways of thinking.

Some seeds fell among thorns. In this example, persons hear the good news of Christ and accept it. Outwardly, they say and do things that imply they have embraced a life for Christ. Often we encounter them in church. But, life challenges and possibly the deceitfulness of wealth choke their new-found belief in Christ. Sometimes they stop attending church; but, even when they continue to attend, their life doesn't produce fruit for Christ. Ananias and Sapphira are an example of seed that fell among thorns (Acts 5:1-11). This husband and wife were Christian converts in the early Jerusalem church. Both were swayed by desire for admiration and prestige to lie to church leaders about the amount of money they were paid for a field they sold.

Some seed fell on good soil and this soil was deep enough for the plant to develop a good root structure and retain water for the plant to grow. If and when thorns sprung up around this plant, it was rooted deep enough that it didn't succumb to the thorns and cares of the world. This plant produced a crop of fruit for Christ. Not all plants produced the same amount of fruit, that is, some produced 30, some produced 60, and others produced 100 times what was sown, but all produced fruit. Early church leaders such as Paul, Titus, Priscilla, and Aquila are Bible examples of seed that fell on good soil.

According to the Hebrews' writer, land that produces thorns and thistles is worthless and in danger of being cursed. Ananias and Sapphira were members of the Jerusalem community of Christians. They made a profession of faith in Christ. Likely, both were baptized. Perhaps, both had the Holy Spirit imputed to them either at Pentecost or by apostles laying hands on them. Yet, Satan filled both of their hearts. Both died unrepentant. When they lied about the payment for the field they sold, they crucified Christ all over again and certainly subjected Christ to public disgrace.

****

What is the effect of rain on a thorn-infested field?

1. Will increasing the amount of rain that falls on the thorn-infested land cause the land to produce good crops? What will happen when the thorn-infested land receives more rain?

2. What happens to thorn infested land if a farmer adds fertilizer to the soil? Will fertilizer on the thorn-infected land cause good crops to grow there?

3. What should a farmer do with a thorn-filled field?

****

Thorns were first mentioned in Genesis as a way God cursed the ground when he expelled Adam and Eve from Eden. Thorns grew on the acacia tree in the Sinai desert and on Jotham's thorn tree in the Promised Land. Isaiah warned Ahaz that the land around Jerusalem would become thorn infested because of his disobedience. In the Sermon on the Mount, Jesus asked if people can pick grapes from thorn bushes.

The Mediterranean buckthorn is a slow growing thornbush common in the Mediterranean Basin where Jewish converts lived in the first century Christian church. The buckthorn is an unattractive shrub that doesn't normally grow in cultivated gardens or fields. It prefers to grow in poor soil that is gritty and highly eroded. Along with the thistle, the buckthorn is the last species to disappear when livestock over-grazed an area. I wonder if the Hebrews writer is telling us that individuals like Ananias and Sapphira often continue to attend church and fellowship despite their secret rejection of Christian beliefs and production of thorns.

Most gardeners and farmers don't view the Mediterranean buckthorn as attractive or desirable. Buckthorn is tangled and many branched. Grayish stems are topped with thorny spikes. Small flowers are yellowish and inconspicuous. Initially green, fruit turns black when mature. Although birds like the fruit, humans find it bitter. The buckthorn fruit is an emetic and laxative. In large quantities fruits are toxic to humans. Certainly Christians don't want to consume buckthorn fruit.

Aphids are attracted to the Mediterranean buckthorn. If the buckthorn grows in a damp climate, it tends to develop a fungal disease. Once aphids and fungus appear on plants, they often spread to more valuable plants in the area. Similarly, church-attending, seeming Christian individuals with negative thoughts or wrong doctrine can spread their beliefs to others in the community of believers. Like the Mediterranean buckthorn, they have no value. The parable suggests that thorn-infested land should be burned as a strategy to remove it. Church leaders need to ponder the optimal way to remove buckthorn from their congregations; they can't allow false doctrine to continue in their congregation.

Buckthorn branches

Buckthorn shrub

Maria Lin

The Hebrew word for thorn (Isaiah 7:23-25) is *shayith* which translates as scrub, thorn, or trash.[1] Trash is debris from plant materials, something worth little or nothing. It should be removed and destroyed (burned) so it doesn't regrow somewhere else. Trash is an excellent symbol for men and women, who learned what Christ did for them, tasted the heavenly gift and goodness of the word of God, shared in the Holy Spirit, and then turned away from the goodness of God. The outcome for these individuals isn't the storehouse of God, but a burning trash heap.

****

The Hebrew word for thorn means trash!

1. What would it take for a fallen individual to re-establish a relationship with Christ?

2. What is the likelihood that a person will re-establish a relationship with Christ after falling away?

3. If you have a loved one who falls away from belief in Christ, what can, or should, you do to try to restore them to Christ?

****

We aren't in Ananias and Sapphira's minds; consequently, we don't know if they were truly converted to Christianity. Acts gives the impression that they completed the Christian "To Do" list, i.e., profession of faith in Christ as Savior, public baptism, indwelling of the Holy Spirit, taking communion (body and blood of Christ), church attendance; but, perhaps they didn't have a personal relationship with Christ. Alternatively, perhaps this early church couple moved deliberately away from Christ. Worldly events became more attractive than Christ. Whatever happened in this couple's lives, we don't want the same thing to happen to us. We don't want to crucify Christ anew or subject him to public disgrace. We don't want to die unrepentant.

Final Thoughts:
Do you know anyone who was a believer, then rejected Jesus. Afterward, they returned to Jesus a second time? How was their witness for Jesus viewed in the non-religious community?

Chapter 23
Grass in the Field

Getting Started: Read 1 Peter 1:23-26

In Jesus's Sermon on the Mount, he included the parable of lilies adorning grass. In contrast to Jesus's emphasis on flowers, Peter's parable mentioned flowers, but focused on field grass. Peter encourages Christians to live a holy life because their physical life on earth is short and then comes a great reward. Belief and hope in Jesus means eternal spiritual life with him. Peter reminded Christians that they were born again through belief in the enduring Word of God. The enduring Word of God is Jesus (John 1:1-5). In his letter, Peter quoted almost verbatim from a parable given initially by the prophet Isaiah. Here is what Peter wrote: "All men are like grass, and all their glory is like the flowers of the field; the grass withers and the flowers fall, but the word of the Lord stands forever" (1 Peter 1:24 NIV).

Most scholars agree that Silas acted as Peter's secretary and carried this letter to Christians in what is now inland Turkey. In his first letter, Peter draws comparisons between the transience of field grass and the brevity of mankind's life. The transiency of life is a common theme in the Bible. Both King David and Isaiah compared man to grass which soon withers and dies away (Psalm 37:2; Psalm 103:15; Isaiah 40:6).

This year, the Roanoke Valley received an overabundance of rain. We are in the month of December and grass is still green. Yet, I remember when I lived in San Francisco. Sometimes, I drove over the Golden Gate Bridge and

traveled up Highway 80 into the Sacramento Valley. June through August, and even into September and October, the grass along the highway was brown and appeared dead.

****

Some of my days go fast. Others seem to drag!

1. Why do so many Bible writers describe life as short? Short in comparison to what? Does your years seem shorter and shorter as you age. Why or why not?

2. Did you learn in school Edna St. Vincent Millay's words: "My candle burns at both ends; it will not last the night; but ah, my foes, and oh, my friends – it gives a lovely light!"[9] How do you think this small poem relates to physical life?

3. Look up the definition of an annual and a perennial plant? Which type of plant do you most identify with? If you had a choice of being an annual or a perennial plant, which would you chose?

****

In first century Palestine, there were scores of grasses in the local flora. One of the most valuable native grass species was known as orchard grass. Orchard grass grew wild on hill sides and in shallow areas, in both sun and shade. Most likely orchard grass covered the large slopes where crowds set to listen to Jesus's sermons and smaller areas where Jesus took Peter and other disciples for private talks. Rains came October through March. In those months, grass was green and carpeted the hills. As spring progressed into summer, grass turned brown from the scorching heat of the sun and lack of rain. Grass and wildflowers dried and turned into brown straw.

Orchard grass is a perennial plant. That means that even through it dies in the summer, grass regrows the following year. Orchard grass produces a flower head called a panicle. Seeds are produced in the flower heads. Initially, seeds are green, but, turn brown as they mature; then, seeds drop to the ground. Although some seeds are carried away by the wind and others eaten by birds, most remain where they drop. Seeds enter the soil, germinate when it rains, and regrow the following year.

Grass of the field   Maria Lin

Peter told the Christians that they were born again with imperishable seed—the word of God (1 Peter 1:23). In the Bible, the Word of God is the living Christ. St. John wrote that in the beginning was the Word and the Word was with God and the Word was God (John 1:1). Christians are born again by believing that Jesus is God's son and Savior of the world. In his physical body, Jesus died on the cross.

Most living men and women will die unless Jesus returns to earth first. After physical death, Jesus rose from the dead. Individuals who believe in Jesus and who die physically will rise again. Why—because they are born again with the imperishable seed of belief in the Word of God (1 Peter 1:23).

****

As a Christian, you are born with imperishable seed!

1. How are Christian men and women perishable?

2. How are Christian men and women imperishable?

3. Differentiate between the physical you and the spiritual you.

****

King David, Isaiah, Peter, and Jesus made the point that life is transient by comparing man's life with field grass. They were all correct that grass withers and dies and that physical life is transient; it withers and dies. At the same time, most field grass is a perennial. It withers and dies with the heat of the sun and lack of rain. Most field grass has a deep root structure and it produces seeds which germinate and grow.

Individuals who don't believe that Jesus is the son of God die like field grass at the end of a season. In contrast, we, who are born by the Word of God, have physical lives that wither and die; but, we are perennials. Our root structure is firmly embedded in Jesus. We produce seeds of righteousness. We are going to live with Jesus even after our physical bodies wither and die. As Peter wrote, we are born again, not of perishable seed, but of imperishable seed (1 Peter 1:23).

****

How do we get to be born again so that we never perish?

1. If you aren't sure, read, ponder and explain:

   a. Romans 3:22-23
   b. John 3:16
   c. 1 John 5:11-12

2. Do you need or want to take any action, or are you where you want to be?

****

The New Testament Greek word for grass is *chŏrtŏs* which comes from a word meaning a pasture.[1] Pastures had important meaning to the ancient Israelites. Jeremiah (50:7) wrote that God was the true pasture of the Israelites. King David declared that the Lord is our shepherd and makes us lie down in green pastures (Psalm 23:2). Jesus named himself the good shepherd (John 10:9-14). Sheep only lie down when they feel secure. When sheep feel threatened, they stand up and look around seeking the source of peril. God's sheep never need to feel threatened. With Jesus as our shepherd, we can rest contentedly in green meadows. We don't have to fear life in this world or the next.

Final Thoughts:
Remember when folks describe a good life as being in "deep cotton?" Are you living spiritually in "deep cotton?"

Chapter 24
Wormwood, Plant and a Shooting Star

Getting Started: Read Revelation 8:10-11

John, the Apostle, is the writer of Revelation. He recorded a vision that involved angels, one after the other, blowing trumpets. With the sounding of each trumpet, something occurred on earth. When an angel sounded the third trumpet, a star, blazing like a torch, fell to Earth. The name of the blazing star was Wormwood. Wormwood is a plant, more specifically a bitter herb.

When the first trumpet was sounded, a mixture of hail, fire, and blood was hurled down onto the earth. The result was a major ecological catastrophe; one third of trees and one third of green grasses were scorched. When an angel sounded the second trumpet, something like a huge blazing mountain was thrown into the sea. The result was that one third of the sea creatures died and one third of ships were destroyed.

The result of both trumpets unleased devastation on the world; however, the sounding of the third trumpet was significant in that for the first time John recorded that people died from the effect of the trumpet sounding. Wormwood, the falling star, caused one third of earth's fresh waters to turn bitter. Many people died from drinking the bitter waters.

****

Bitterness is harmful or destructive to our soul,
which is composed of our mind, emotions, and will.

1. Your will encompasses your disposition, inclinations, passions, appetite, even your desires. It is how you customarily act. How can your will be influenced by bitterness, and poisoned by how you live your life?

2. If you don't like or want bitterness in your life, what strategies can you implement to remove it from your life?

3. Identify at least one strategy that you will start implementing today.

****

Perhaps 21st century, more than first century, readers can relate to John's vision of a star falling to earth and contaminating one third of the earth's fresh water. We understand that the planet Earth isn't alone in the cosmos. Celestial events have, do, and will impact our planet and lives. When we read about a star falling to earth, we think of a meteorite (children call them shooting stars) or a comet that enters earth's atmosphere and lands on the earth. If the celestial traveler doesn't burn up as it passes through the earth's atmosphere, the falling star is large.

Moving from a falling meteorite or comet to bitter water requires deductive thought. Perhaps, the cosmic traveler contains contaminated particles released as it moved through the earth's atmosphere. When contaminated particles fall to the earth, they poison fresh water. An alternative explanation is that when the meteor lands on the earth's surface, it sends dust into the air. If the earth's surface contains high levels of pollutants, pollutants rise into the atmosphere. With the rotation of the earth and wind patterns, polluted particles spread around the globe. When contaminants fall to the earth's surface, they contaminate rivers, lakes, streams, and other fresh water used for drinking.

The recipients of John's letter understood the significance of one third of the fresh water turning bitter. Mankind needs fresh water to live. Although a person can live 21 days without food, few can live more than 3-5 days without water when the temperature is about 70-degree Fahrenheit. In tropical areas where temperatures are substantially higher or in extremely dry climates like in the Middle East, individuals survive less time without fresh water. Thirsty people will do one of two things: die from dehydration or drink the contaminated water and die from its poison.

****

Currently, a United States city has a contaminated water supply. Despite the water's appearance, city officials assured residents the water was drinkable. Adults drank it, cooked with it, and gave it to their children. They are poisoned.

****

Bitter water wasn't a new idea to early Christian Jews, even Gentile Christians. Most knew every step of the Israelites exodus from Egypt. They remembered that three days after the Israelites left Egypt they arrived at the spring at Marah in the Desert of Shur. At Marah, the Israelites expected to find fresh water; instead the water was bitter and undrinkable. The Bible didn't identify what made the Marah spring water undrinkable; however, Moses's action provided a clue. God told Moses to throw a piece of wood into the spring. Jewish rabbis believe the wood was from a mangrove tree, one of the few trees that leaches saline from water.[10] The result was that the Marah spring water became drinkable. The reverse of the miracle at Marah happens in John's parable: instead of bitter water becoming sweet, sweet water became bitter. In Revelation, God's action of causing Wormwood to fall on earth was to get people's attention and cause repentance.

Although the Hebrew word for wormwood (*laanah*)[1] is used about eight times in the Old Testament, in the New Testament the name Wormwood is used only for this blazing star in Revelations. In the Old Testament, wormwood is synonymous with a bitter taste or poison. It was used as a metaphor for Israelites' idolatry, calamity and sorrow, and false judgments. In reality, wormwood is an herb, native to the eastern Mediterranean area to include Canaan/Palestine. With the exception of rue, wormwood was the bitterest herb known in ancient

Wormwood   Maria Lin

times. Wormwood is an appropriate name for a blazing star that contaminates fresh water and brings death to millions of earth's people.

Similar to the bitter feelings which occur and reoccur after loved ones die, the plant wormwood regrows year after year; it is a perennial. Ancient people believed that if wormwood was hung to dry, it couldn't be placed in full sun or its aromatic properties would be lost. In contrast to many plants that thrive in sunny locations, wormwood prefers to grow in the shade. In earlier centuries, a shade was a ghost, a disembodied spirit. Often shades appeared in dimly lighted locations. The shade-loving properties of common wormwood echo the pall and moral decay that was endemic in ancient Israel and Judah before the nations were conquered. Both nations worshiped idols and foreign gods.

Spiritually, John's visions depicted events near the end of the ages. The purpose of these calamities and judgements on earth was to cause mankind to repent. Imagine the effects of the first three judgements on the earth: qne third of trees and plants destroyed, scarce food, maritime trade curtailed with destruction of one-third of the earth's ships. Many luxury items from foreign countries will be unavailable i.e., spices, technological items, fruits, and vegetables. Oil imported to heat homes, fuel vehicles, and support manufacturing will be reduced substantially. When we turn on a water faucet, water may be undrinkable. Family and neighbors will die. People will be sorrowful and bitter over loss of life and loss of their livelihood. Our spirits will be overwhelmed.

****

"At the deepest level our spirit gives us meaning and purpose and our spirit enables us to love one another, our self, and God. It's through our spirit that we have communion and fellowship with God."[11]

1. Is there anything in your spiritual life that you don't think is ideal or that you want to improve?

2. What are some strategies that you could use to improve your spiritual life, to improve your spirit?

3. Identify at least one strategy you will start today—and follow through on— to enhance your spiritual life.

****

When the seven seals were opened and the trumpets sounded millions of earth's people died. Think of the bitterness these deaths causes on individuals who lost loved ones. Despite the severity of God's judgements, mankind refused to repent of their sins and acknowledge God as sovereign. The Bible says that people continued to worship demons and idols (Revelation 9:20-21). What does God have to do to get mankind's attention and cause mankind to repent of sins?

Final Thoughts:
How does personal bitterness poison us,
i.e., our thoughts, words, and character?

References

1. Strong, James. *The New Strong's exhaustive concordance of the Bible*. Nashville, TN: Thomas Nelson Publishers, 2010.

2. Hareuveni, Nogah, and Helen Frenkley. *Tree and shrub in our biblical heritage*. Kiryat Ono, Israel: Neot Kedumim Limited, 1989.

3. Modzelevich, Martha. *Flowers in Israel*. http://www.flowersinisrael.com, 2016.

4. Adeyemo, Tokunboh, ed. *Africa Bible commentary*. Grand Rapids, MI: Zondervan, 2006.

5. MacDonald, William. *Believer's Bible commentary*. Nashville, TN: Thomas Nelson Publishers, 1995.

6. Lockyer, Herbert. *All the parables in the Bible*. Grand Rapids, MI: Zondervan, 1963.

7. Borowski, Oded. *Agriculture in iron age Israel*. Winona Lake, IN: Eisenbrauns, 2009.

8. Whiston, William. *The Works of Josephus, Complete and Unabridged*. Peabody, MA, Hendrickson Publishers Inc., 1987.

9. Millay. Edna St. Vincent. *First fig. A few figs from thistles*. New York, NY: Harper & Brothers, 1922.

10. Rabinowitz, Louis I. *Torah and flora*. New York, NY: Sanhedrin Press, 1977.

11.   Faith and Health Connection, Teaching biblical truths for health and wellness.   http://www.faithandhealthconnection.org, 2016.

List of Illustrations

Made in the USA
Monee, IL
25 September 2020